BELONGING
AND
BANISHMENT

Being Muslim in Canada

edited by

Natasha Bakht

© 2008 the authors

Except for purposes of review, no part of this
book may be reproduced in any form without
prior permission of the publisher.

We acknowledge the support of
the Canada Council for the Arts for our publishing program.

  Canada Council   Conseil des Arts   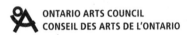   ONTARIO ARTS COUNCIL
for the Arts   du Canada   CONSEIL DES ARTS DE L'ONTARIO

We also acknowledge support from
the Government of Ontario through the Ontario Arts Council.

Cover design by David Drummond
Author photo by Michael Slobodian

Library and Archives Canada Cataloguing in Publication

    Belonging and banishment : being Muslim in Canada / [edited by]
Natasha Bakht.

Includes bibliographical references.
ISBN 978-1-894770-48-4

    1. Muslims--Canada--Social conditions. 2. Muslims--Canada.
I. Bakht, Natasha, 1972-

FC106.M9B44 2008   305.6'970971   C2008-906613-8

Printed in Canada by Coach House Printing

TSAR Publications
P. O. Box 6996, Station A
Toronto, Ontario M5W 1X7
Canada

www.tsarbooks.com

TABLE OF CONTENTS

Introduction   v
NATASHA BAKHT

Muslims and the Rule of Law   1
HAROON SIDDIQUI

Bearing the Name of the Prophet   17
SYED MOHAMED MEHDI

Knowing the Universe in All its Conditions   26
ARIF BABUL

Raising Muslim Children in a Diverse World   43
RUKHSANA KHAN

Islamic Theology and Moral Agency:
Beyond the Pre- and Post-Modern   51
ANVER M EMON

Muslim Girl Magazine:
Representing Ourselves   62
AUSMA ZEHANAT KHAN

Towards a Dialogical Discourse for Canadian Muslims   74
AMIN MALAK

Islamic Authority:
Changing Expectations Among Canadian Muslims   85
KARIM H KARIM

A Case of Mistaken Identity:
Inside and Outside the Muslim Ummah   99
ANAR ALI

Victim or Aggressor?
Typecasting Muslim Women for their Attire   105
NATASHA BAKHT

Politics Over Principles:
The Case of Omar Khadr   114
SHEEMA KHAN

NOTES   129
BIBLIOGRAPHY   141
CONTRIBUTORS   144

Introduction

NATASHA BAKHT

When I was six or seven most of my friends from school had no idea what a Muslim was. To say that you were a Muslim usually drew a blank stare. I didn't know enough then to try to explain what it meant to be a Muslim. As I got older, I remember distinctly hearing much talk of the "religion Muslim." I was always terribly impressed by the odd person who knew the difference between the religion and those who practised it. As a young adult, I was disconcerted to discover that, in fact, many people knew or thought they knew what Islam was and who Muslims were. This discovery has been a painful one fraught with anger, sadness, guilt, heartache, and fear. This book is an attempt to do what I couldn't as a child, that is, to explain who a Muslim might be and to consider the issues that are of importance to Muslims.

And no wonder a child would have trouble. Contrary to most portrayals of Muslims in popular culture, we are not a monolithic group of people with a singular preoccupation. The intention of this book is to represent, in a thoughtful and nuanced manner, the diversity of Muslims in Canada, the issues that are of importance to them, and the problems that are thrust upon them. The book is by no means an exhaustive representation of Muslims and their views. I doubt any collection of works could manage that. But the contributors to this book in their divergent choice of topics and professional and personal leanings confirm that diversities amongst Muslims are pronounced and worthy of serious acknowledgement and celebration.

Although the contributors to this book were given free reign with respect to subject matter, several interesting themes have emerged. As the title of this collection suggests, the authors' experiences of being in Canada, their understanding of the Islamic *ummah,* or community, and their insights into the roles and responsibilities of Muslims, the media, the government, and the general public have produced a dual (though not binary) approach to their relationship with Canada and the debates that occur within it. If one imagines the ideas of belonging and banishment to appear along a spectrum, then each contributor would likely place himself or herself in a different position, depending on the topic, closer or further away from either end. This staking of positions would not necessarily be a binary process as they may even experience belonging and banishment simultaneously.

This collection on one hand conveys a picture of Muslims assaulted by the numerous discriminatory responses to terrorism prevalent in Canada, including outright human rights violations (Siddiqui, Bakht, S Khan). It also offers a portrait of Canada, with its protection of multiculturalism embedded in the *Canadian Charter of Rights and Freedoms,* as a haven from unjust and undemocratic regimes (Malak). It provides a complex idea of Muslims by illustrating disagreements within and between the many Muslim communities about a number of important issues (Emon, A Khan, Ali, Karim). And finally it presents narratives steeped in history; the history of previous generations, of great Muslim philosophers, poets, architects, musicians, and scientists and the importance of passing this history and its lessons on to future generations (Mehdi, Babul, R Khan). Belonging and banishment take on very different connotations in each of these contexts.

Some contributors level criticism at "moderate Muslims," the attention that they garner from the conventional media for towing the mainstream line by disparaging other Muslims and the narrow vision of the kinds of views Muslims can and ought to have (Siddiqui, Mehdi, Ali). This collection attempts to create a space for Muslim voices less heard.

Issues involving Muslim women are raised – the impact of their dress, their right to be free from violence, their claims of equality and religious freedom, and the appropriation of their stories by the media and others (Siddiqui, A Khan, Malak, Ali, Bakht). The status of Muslim women in Canada and elsewhere is an area of research that has garnered much attention. I have little doubt that the authors in this collection are in agreement that women's rights are critical to the healthy development of any democracy. These chapters probe the more difficult questions of how one continues to advance equality, without furthering intolerance (but remaining self-critical) and what equality might mean in a country as pluralistic as ours.

Some commonalities that recur in these pages include the view that generally many Canadians do not know enough about Muslims or Islam and that what they do understand is driven by inaccurate mainstream descriptions (A Khan, Ali, Mehdi). The chapters in this book provide a counterpoint to misapprehensions about Islam and typical media depictions of Muslims. A number of the authors make comparisons to other communities, such as the Japanese Canadians, who have been targeted and subject to grave oppression during other perceived crises of security (Siddiqui, Malak, S Khan). These comparisons present important opportunities for alliance-building, a vital element in the struggle for justice.

Haroon Siddiqui, editorial page editor emeritus and columnist for the *Toronto Star*, provides a comprehensive review of certain events of the past several years that indicate that Islamophobia has reared its ugly head in Canada. Siddiqui warns that deviations from the rule of law will not only affect Muslims in Canada but also erode the country's most fundamental democratic principles.

Syed Mohamed Mehdi, professor of philosophy and a musician, has written a personal yet deeply political piece on bearing the name of the prophet. This chapter is rich in descriptive detail, with many hints of humour, and suggests that the portrait of a Muslim is not bound up in outward symbols but is one infused with the goals of social justice and other progressive ideals.

Arif Babul, professor of physics and astronomy at the University of Victoria, provides a fascinating account of how one devout man reconciles his faith with his professional scientific pursuits. The reader is taken through a very compelling deconstruction of the archetypal conflicts between science and religion, to discover that the author, like other well-known scientists, comfortably occupies both of these realms.

Rukhsana Khan, a writer of children's books, affords us a unique glimpse into her own childhood and the upbringing of her children.

Her account of raising religious children while insisting that they attend public schools is a thoughtful example of giving children the tools to make appropriate choices. It is also implicitly an important discourse on how public institutions can assist and accommodate religious parents and children.

Anver Emon, professor of law at the University of Toronto, introduces the reader to the question of free will and determinism through premodern debates within Islamic theology. These debates are framed within the larger question of moral agency, that is, how one finds meaning in life. In addition to being a very lively illustration of early Islamic discussions and disagreements about moral agency, this chapter advocates that the relevance of understanding one tradition's perspectives can resonate with similar investigations of moral meaning today.

Ausma Khan is the Editor-in-Chief of the very successful and unique *Muslim Girl* magazine. Her chapter details the reasons behind the creation of this publication, including the reality that young Muslim girls are very much a part of the North American landscape. In presenting the multiple and wide-ranging stories and images of girls who self-identify as Muslims and in underscoring their roles in the arts, one is assured that creating honest, trendy, stimulating work about and for young Muslims is possible indeed.

Amin Malak, professor of English at Grant MacEwan College, writes of a dialogical discourse for Canadian Muslims. He chronicles several significant areas of interest to Muslims and other Canadians attracted to the idea of sustaining a rich, equality-seeking and pluralistic society. This chapter offers the hope of an ever more tolerant and reciprocal country, but not without insisting on accountability.

Karim H Karim, the director of Carleton University's School of Journalism and Communication, presents very interesting research about the way some Muslims are reformulating the criteria required for competent Islamic authority in Canada. This chapter, based on focus group research in three different countries, tracks the distinct changes and developments in contemporary conditions in the West that have altered some Muslims' relationships with religious authorities.

Anar Ali's demand for specificity in discussions about Muslims and Islam is a valuable lesson for those researching and writing about

Muslim communities. In her essay about mistaken identities, she comments on the multiple worlds that Muslims like herself straddle and the unique perspectives they can offer to those both inside and outside Muslim communities.

My own piece tackles the seemingly ubiquitous issue of Muslim women's dress, but entirely within the Canadian context. The case studies of Muslim women and girls who are prohibited from wearing the hijab in certain employment and sports contexts are contrasted with efforts to prohibit niqab-wearing women from voting without showing their faces. In the first instance, such prohibitions are rationalized as protections for Muslim women and girls while in the latter, these prohibitions are needed to protect Canadians from Muslim women.

Sheema Khan, columnist for the *Globe and Mail*, provides Canadians with a much-needed exposition of the tragic case of Omar Khadr, the minor who has been subjected to torture and detained in the demeaning conditions of Guantanamo Bay for the past six years. Khan delineates the numerous failures of successive Canadian governments to fight for the rights of Omar Khadr. Notwithstanding the discomfort felt by many Muslim Canadians about the terrorist leanings of the Khadr family, Khan courageously argues that Omar Khadr cannot be the scapegoat for his family's beliefs or actions.

The chapters in this book begin to answer the question of who a Muslim might be. The contributors to this collection in their diversity and with their impressive talents have begun to challenge what one ordinarily hears about Muslims. Their views are varied and perhaps even contradictory, but the richness of the critical exchange of ideas that they propose is a refreshing call for change.

Muslims and the Rule of Law

HAROON SIDDIQUI

There is nothing that more closely resembles anti-Semitism than Islamophobia. Both have the same face: that of stupidity and hate.
— NICOLAS SARKOZY, President of France

Canada has not been immune from post-9/11 Islamophobia and the politics of fear. I say this not so much to echo the episodic Muslim discourse of victimology but as a Canadian saddened by the impact of anti-Muslim prejudice on the Canadian polity, whose defining premise is the equality of all people living under one law, uniformly applied.

In support of this proposition, the following episodes jump to mind:

- The Maher Arar tragedy.
- The alleged Canadian complicity in the reported torture in Syria of three other Canadian Arabs.
- The sad saga of five Arabs caught in the dragnet of the federal security certificates.
- The 2003 mistaken arrest of 23 Muslim men of Pakistani and Indian origin in Toronto as "suspected terrorists," but against whom not a single terrorism-related charge was laid.
- The 2006 arrest of 18 Toronto-area Muslims on terrorism-related charges, a case so poorly formulated that charges had to be dropped against as many as seven of the accused even before the trial began.

Terrorism is for real; it cannot be wished away. The only democratic debate is over how best to combat it – within the rule of law, fairly applied, or outside of it, as in George W Bush's "war on terror," waged mostly outside of international and domestic legal frameworks. Canada being Canada, it alone among Western nations established a royal commission to probe a post-9/11 injustice, namely the Arar case, and offered him an official apology and financial compensation for Canadian complicity in his torture. Ottawa also appointed a former Supreme Court judge, the Hon Frank Iacobucci, to inquire into the plight of the three other Arabs who allegedly suffered the same fate as Arar. He concluded that all three were indeed tortured in Damascus, with official Canadian complicity, albeit indirect (Iacobucci, 36–39). And the Supreme Court unanimously declared the security certificates to be unconstitutional. Still, all that was of little or no comfort to those wrongly maligned and tarred for life as "terrorists." Nor could it obscure the reality that anti-Muslim bigotry has been very much in evidence in several public policy debates and decisions:

- The highly charged and falsely labeled sharia controversy in Ontario in 2005–06.
- The public backlash during the 2007 Ontario election against the Conservative Party's proposal to extend public funding to Protestant, Jewish, Hindu, Muslim and other religious schools, along the same lines as already given to Catholic schools.
- The Harper government's crude attempts in 2007 at banning niqabi women from voting.
- The 2007–08 "reasonable accommodation" debate in Quebec which was anything but.
- The disbarring of hijabi girls from sundry soccer, tae kwon do, and judo competitions.

Muslim-bashing has also become a regular feature of a segment of our mainstream media – the tabloid press in Quebec, and in English Canada, the *National Post* and the other Canwest-controlled group of newspapers (the *Gazette* in Montreal, the *Ottawa Citizen*, the *Regina Leader-Post*, the *Saskatoon Star Phoenix*, the *Calgary Herald*, the *Edmonton Journal*, the *Vancouver Sun*, and the *Province*), and

Maclean's, "Canada's national magazine." Complaints against the latter, filed by a group of Muslims before the federal as well as the Ontario and British Columbia human rights commissions, evinced a storm of protest, unlike any seen during similar cases filed by other groups before the same commissions.

The pattern of coverage by these media outlets is now familiar. They hold up the bad behaviour of a few Muslims as symptomatic of all. They emphasize the words and deeds of fringe militants and radicals, while ignoring the overwhelming majority of law-abiding Muslims, except for "moderate Muslims" who criticize fellow-Muslims and Islam. The media also express selective outrage about the plight of Muslim women. As Pankaj Mishra, Indian essayist and novelist, writes: "Almost every day newspaper columnists berate Islam, often couching their prejudice in the highly moral language of women's rights."

Controversies are the lifeblood of democracy. But they also provide useful insights into prevailing prejudices, and who exploits them.

Sharia Arbitration and Religious Schools

Let's be honest: No sharia law could possibly have come to Canada, even if some of its proponents foolishly thought so, and its critics happily fanned fears against it and the media gleefully sensationalized it. Rather, the crux of the matter was Ontario's 1991 *Arbitration Act* – specifically, whether that law applied equally to all religions. Christians and Jews had been practising religiously informed arbitration in business disputes and such family matters as the division of marital assets, with little or no public opposition. But no sooner had a small group of Muslims declared their intention to do the same than hysteria broke out, leaving no room for a rational discussion on why some Muslims may want to have their family law disputes dealt with according to religious principles, just as some Jews preferred to take their issues to a Beit din. It also did not seem to matter that all decisions taken under the *Arbitration Act* could easily be made compatible with Canadian law by subjecting them to appeal in the regular courts, as Marion Boyd, former Attorney-General of Ontario and a staunch feminist, suggested in a report commissioned by Queen's Park (Boyd, 135). As Professor Will Kymlicka of Queen's University, Canada's leading theoretician on multiculturalism, was to write later, the suggestion that sharia was going to trump Canadian law was "a complete misrepresentation" (Kymlicka, 153). It could also not be credibly argued that Canadian Muslim women faced any more pressure to conform than Catholic or Jewish women in matters of, say, annulment or *get*, the Jewish divorce.

The Ontario government thus had no choice but to either allow such arbitration for all faith groups or for none. Queen's Park opted for the latter, picking the relatively easier of the two hard political choices.

If Premier Dalton McGuinty was stumped by sharia, Tory leader John Tory lost an election over his promise to fund all faith-based schools. If public unease with Muslims and Islam was blatant in the sharia controversy, it was implicit, though not all that hidden, in the case of funding for religious schools. While not all opposition to the latter was driven by the fear of Islamic schools, much of it was, as candidates from the election trenches readily attested.

The victims in both cases were not just Ontario Muslims – the handful who had asked for religious arbitration or the few hundreds who were hoping for financial support for educating their children in Islamic schools. Far more numerous were the Christians, Jews, and others who had been using religious arbitration for 15 years (1991–2006), and the parents of about 53,000 children enrolled in Protestant, Jewish, Hindu, Sikh and other faith schools.

I happen to oppose both religious-based arbitration and funding for faith-based schools. But regardless of one's position, what we all need to think about is this: when a mature democracy like ours cannot debate faith-related issues in a rational manner, we have a problem.

Quebec's Spasm of Bigotry

The code of conduct for immigrants approved in January, 2007 by the town council of Herouxville – Thou shall not stone women to death or circumcise them, nor wear the hijab or carry the kirpan in public, nor expect employers to provide a place or time off for prayers, etc. (Levesque) – was initially greeted with amused indifference. After all, the town of 1,300, located 160 miles north-east of Montreal, had only one immigrant family and wasn't going to attract many others, especially after its burst of bigotry. But it soon became clear that the town's sentiments had resonance well beyond its boundaries.

A Montreal police officer's anti-immigrant song, *That's Enough Already*, was gaining currency: *We want to accept ethnics/but not at any price. If you're not happy with your fate/there's a place called the airport* (CP 1). The popular press was in a tizzy over incidents involving Orthodox Jews and Muslims: A downtown Montreal yeshiva had got the next-door YMCA to agree to tint its windows, so as not to tempt the young students to gawk at women exercising in tights. A group of Muslims had ostensibly forced a rural maple syrup farm to take the ham out of pea soup, Quebec's culinary Holy Grail, and had commandeered the dancehall for their prayers.

In the provincial election that followed in March 2007, Mario Dumont, the leader of the Action Démocratique du Québec, campaigned against immigrants and minorities, especially Muslims. Not to be left behind, the Parti Quebecois skewered the province's chief electoral officer for his decision to allow women wearing a niqab or burqa to vote. Marcel Blanchet had, in fact, worked out a compromise – the women would have to show their face but only if their identity was in doubt. But politicians were in no mood for any compromise with Muslims, and forced him to reverse himself. The same scenario was played out a few months later, during three federal by-elections in Quebec, when Prime Minister Harper insisted that women had to remove their veils, despite the fact that there was no requirement in the federal law for voters to show their faces.

During these controversies, Premier Jean Charest remained silent. In fact, one of his incumbent Liberal candidates, Fatima Houda-Pepin, played her own anti-Muslim card, claiming that two imams in her riding in the Montreal suburb of Brossard had ordered the faithful not to vote for her. That evoked the perfect cliché of male religious leaders trying to railroad a modern secular Muslim woman. But one of the people she was referring to, Moin Ghauri, who volunteers as a part-time imam, told me in a telephone interview that all he had done was to express his own opinion – that, too, in response to a query by a reporter – that he personally would not vote for her. He had definitely not said that Houda-Pepin was "a bad Muslim," as she had claimed, but rather that she had been a bad member of the National Assembly, in that she rarely talked to Muslims, whom she was often deriding. As the sole Muslim member of the National Assembly, she had been selected during Ontario's sharia controversy to lead a symbolic vote in the Assembly against the proposal. She was, of course, entitled to her view, but one can't imagine any government in North America or Europe using a Catholic or a Jew to lead a vote against the rights of fellow-Catholics or fellow-Jews.

Charest tried to diffuse the raging controversies around "reasonable accommodation" by naming a commission, co-chaired by eminent academics Charles Taylor and Gerard Bouchard, who were to hold hearings well after the election. The tactic, however, did not save the Liberals, who were reduced on election night to a minority, while Dumont emerged as the leader of the opposition. It was the first time in contemporary Canada that an anti-immigrant, anti-minority party had been so amply rewarded. Clearly something was afoot in Quebec.

That became crystal clear when Taylor and Bouchard opened their hearings in the fall. Day after day, witnesses spewed anti-Semitic and anti-Islamic vitriol. They had a litany of complaints: some public swimming pools were setting aside women-only hours for Muslims; some schools were providing space for prayers; junior hockey star Benjamin Rubin of the Gatineau Olympique was absenting himself on Saturdays for the Sabbath; Montreal's Jewish General Hospital staff had ejected an ambulance driver from its cafeteria for eating a ham sandwich, etc. Others added such gems as, "Would you like to see your grandchildren become Muslim? Would you like to see your granddaughters wear the veil?" (Ha 1) and, "It's gotten to the point where 33 per cent of (Supreme Court) judges are Jewish" (Ha 2).

This prompted the suggestion that Quebecers were becoming xenophobic. That was not entirely a correct reading. The 2006 census data showed that immigrants accounted for 11.5 per cent of the province's population, a historic high. Between 2001 and 2006, Quebec had welcomed immigrants at a faster pace than the country as a whole (a 20.5 per cent increase vs. 13.6 per cent). Montreal had attracted more immigrants than Vancouver (165,300 vs. 151,700). A significant number of immigrants to Quebec were Muslims.

No, Quebecers didn't so much mind immigrants and minorities as they wanted to dictate the terms under which such people could live in Quebec – an assimilationist ethos out of date by a quarter of a century, as though there had been no *Charter of Rights* and no constitutional multiculturalism. Many Quebecers were clearly pining for the old hierarchical structure, based on the European political and social construct: minorities had better follow majority mores. As several witnesses told the commission, minorities "must adopt Quebec's values," and "conform to our way of life." Orthodox Jews and observant Muslims, in particular, were seen as an affront to the secular and hedonistic kingdom of post-Quiet Revolution Quebec, free at last of the iron grip of the Catholic Church. The kippa and the hijab and the strict sexual code of some Jews and Muslims reminded Quebecers of the religiosity they had rejected decades ago.

Yet the complainants were not equal-opportunity offenders; a majority left little doubt that their chief complaint was with Muslims. Interestingly, the most vehement were the more educated and "liberal" witnesses, such as labour leaders and feminists. These sophisticated bigots wrapped their views in the tinsel of Quebec nationalism, secularism, or gender equity.

The Quebec Federation of Labour suggested that Quebec being secular, state employees – such as doctors, judges, lawyers and police officers – should dress "neutrally." Did that mean that nuns would be banned from public payroll? Or, lawyers wearing a yarmulke or a turban barred from court? The federation wasn't sure but union leader Claudette Carbonneau was certain that "I wouldn't want to see a judge in a veil" (Heinrich).

Christiane Pelchat, president of the Quebec Council on the Status of Women and a former Liberal member of the Assembly, said the niqab sends "a message of the submission of a woman" (Bielski). Lise Bourgault, mayor of Brownsburg-Chatham and a former Tory MP, said laws should be changed to stop "submissive (Muslim) women walking behind their husbands" (Levesque). Apparently there is no room in these feminists' universe for the sovereignty of a Muslim woman to make her own choice of dress. Pelchat: "You cannot limit the equality of the sexes in the name of freedom of religion" (Bielski). Sure. But she was definitely not talking about forcing the Catholic Church to move women parishioners from the pews to the pulpit.

The Media, Especially the *Maclean's* Case

One staple of anti-Semitism has been that Jews have taken over the world, or are about to. Now Muslims are being accused of the same, especially in Europe, where the fear of "Eurabia" is standard fare in Islamophobic circles.

The apocalyptic hypothesis that Muslims pose a dire demographic and ideological threat to the West was introduced in Canada by *Maclean's* magazine in Oct. 2006, in a 4,800-word article entitled "The Future Belongs to Islam." It said:

> Of course, not all Muslims are terrorists – though enough are hot for jihad to provide an impressive support network of mosques from Vienna to Stockholm to Toronto to Seattle. Of course, not all Muslims support terrorists – though enough of them share their basic objectives (the wish to live under Islamic law in Europe and North America) to function wittingly or otherwise as the 'good cop' end of an Islamic good cop/bad cop routine. But, at the very minimum, this fast-moving demographic transformation provides a huge comfort zone for the jihad to move around in.

Of course, the article incensed many Canadians, including four students at York University's Osgoode Hall Law School – Khurrum Awan, Naseem Mithoowani, Muneeza Sheikh, and Ali Ahmed. They counted 18 other anti-Muslim articles in Maclean's, including some by the magazine's columnist Barbara Amiel, wife of Lord Black.

The students met *Maclean's* editor Ken Whyte and deputy editor Mark Stevenson, who were dismissive. The students wrote to owner Ted Rogers, the cable TV mogul. He referred the matter to Brian Segal, the publisher of *Maclean's*, who defended the editor. Not getting anywhere, the students filed complaints with the human rights commissions, arguing that the magazine's writings on Muslims constituted hate speech. Their application had the backing of the Canadian Islamic Congress and later of the Canadian Arab Federation, the Alliance of Concerned Jewish Canadians, the Ontario section of the Canadian Federation of Students and also NDP leader Jack Layton.

The complaint prompted a spate of critical articles and columns in *Maclean's* as well as the *Globe and Mail* and the Canwest newspapers, especially the *National Post*. Some critics tried to undermine the complaint by citing a 2004 comment by Mohamed El Masry, the controversial head of the Canadian Islamic Congress, that all Israeli civilians are fair game for suicide bombers. Most critics, however, invoked the freedom of speech argument, and characterized human rights commissions as "kangaroo courts," which had no business judging media content. But by law, it is the business of human rights commissions to assess and curb hate speech:

- In 1996 and again in 1997, the BC Human Rights Commission ruled against the suburban weekly *North Shore News* for publishing anti-Semitic columns. The writer, Doug Collins, said the verdict was "a direct threat to the freedom of the press" (CP 2).

- In 2002, the federal commission ruled against the notorious Ernst Zundel, ordering him to remove anti-Semitic material from a website. His lawyer, Doug Christie, characterized the ruling as a threat to freedom of speech.

- In 2002, the Alberta Human Rights Commission ruled against the magazine *Alberta Report* for spreading prejudice against Jews. The magazine agreed to give adequate space for a rebuttal. Still, publisher Link Byfield complained about the limits on free expression.

- In December, 2007, the Alberta commission ruled against a Christian pastor, Stephen Boissoin, for a letter published in the

Red Deer Advocate, calling gays "immoral." He protested what he called the suspension of his right to freedom of expression: "I am not allowed to hold on to my views" (Waggoner).

* In 2008, the federal commission probed a complaint against *Catholic Insight* magazine for publishing anti-gay articles. Its editors condemned "the nefarious role of human rights commissions in suppressing freedom of speech" (de Valk).

The pattern is clear. Those hauled before the commissions howl "censorship." But the Supreme Court of Canada has upheld the anti-hate provisions of the *Criminal Code* as well as of the federal and provincial human rights statutes. The court ruled that curbing hate speech is a reasonable and justifiable limit on free expression.

However, several people wanted the law changed. Liberal MP Keith Martin introduced a private member's bill in the House of Commons to delete section 13(1) of the *Canadian Human Rights Act*, which prohibits messages "likely to expose a person or persons to hatred or contempt." Others made similar suggestions regarding provincial codes. This is a legitimate position to adopt. Equally legitimate is the question that follows: Why should we not think of such people as hypocrites, given that they were silent when human rights commissions were ruling on complaints by various groups but got noisy when the complainants were Muslim?

For different reasons, the media, including my own newspaper, the *Toronto Star*, also vehemently oppose human rights tribunals regulating the press. They do so to protect press freedom. They also point to inconsistencies across different Canadian jurisdictions and the grey legal zones created by such technological advances as the Internet.

Not surprisingly, then, only the BC commission decided to hold hearings in the *Maclean's* case, while the federal and Ontario commissions took a pass. The BC commission ruled that the article did not constitute hate, as defined by the commission statutes. But Barbara Hall, chair of the Ontario commission, issued a detailed statement condemning *Maclean's* for Islamophobia. Using the commission's "broader mandate to promote and advance respect for human rights," she wrote:

Islamophobia is a form of racism ... Since September 2001, Islamophobic attitudes are becoming more prevalent and Muslims are increasingly the target of intolerance ... The Maclean's article, and others like it, are examples of this. By portraying Muslims as all sharing the same negative characteristics, including being a threat to "the West," this explicit expression of Islamophobia further perpetuates and promotes prejudice towards Muslims and others.

Her 1,600-word statement, posted on the commission's website, is worth reading in its entirety (http://www.ohrc.on.ca/en/resources/news/macleans). So is a blog by John Miller, veteran journalist and professor of journalism at Ryerson University (http://thejournalism-doctor.ca). He called the *Maclean's* article "xenophobic," and said it was riddled with errors. He ridiculed the Canadian Association of Journalists for its knee-jerk defence, given that the article may have violated the association's own guidelines for fairness, accuracy, access, and antidiscrimination.

One can credibly argue that antihate laws should be made consistent across Canada by exempting the media or axing the antihate provisions altogether from the human rights codes. We may even wish to adopt the American system and remove the antihate section from the *Criminal Code* altogether. But many disagree, including the Canadian Jewish Congress, whose head, Bernie Farber, told me that the antihate laws have helped make Canada "the warm, tolerant and accepting nation that it has become." He noted that there was no outcry when Jewish, gay, and other groups were routinely using the antihate laws but there was the moment Muslims invoked them. "That's really what it's about. When non-Muslims were using it, nobody really cared. People need scapegoats. It used to be Jews. Now it's Muslims."

Beyond the law, there is also common self-restraint. Most media exercise it every day. We do not publish anti-Semitic rants. We routinely reject cartoons that may be unfair or unnecessarily hurtful or racist, which is why readers no longer see the caricatures of savage Aboriginals, fat-lipped Blacks, hook-nosed Jews, or cross-eyed

Chinese. That *Maclean's* published a series of virulent articles about Muslims itself speaks volumes. The self-restraint routinely exercised by the media is all too easily abandoned in the case of Muslims. That was the real issue in the Maclean's case, as it was in the Danish cartoon crisis (2005–06) and as it has been in many similar controversies involving the media and Muslims. For many in the West, freedom of speech has come to mean the freedom to stigmatize Muslims and denigrate many Islamic precepts.

That freedom of speech has limits is recognized even by International PEN, the anticensorship writers' group that is also a leading advocate for freedom of expression. While its charter speaks to the "unhampered transmission of thought," it also insists that "since freedom implies voluntary restraint, members pledge themselves to oppose such evils of a free press as mendacious publication, deliberate falsehood and distortion of facts for political and personal ends." It calls on PEN members to foster "good understanding and mutual respect among nations . . . to do their utmost to dispel race, class and national hatreds, and to champion the ideal of one humanity living in peace in the world (http://www.internationalpen.org.uk/go/about-us/charter)."

The lack of self-restraint on the part of the Quebec media was noted by Taylor and Bouchard. In their final report they accused the media of not only being sensationalist but indeed fomenting the so-called "accommodation crisis," when there wasn't one. "Trivial incidents" had been blown out of proportion. Two commission researchers spent four months reconstructing "21 events that had received the most extensive media coverage and contributed the most to the controversy" (Bouchard and Taylor 69). In as many as 15 cases, they found "striking discrepancies between the version documented during our investigation and the 'stereotyped' version of events" (Bouchard and Taylor 73); and in six cases, they found "striking distortions between general public perceptions and the actual facts" (Bouchard and Taylor 18)." For example, the Muslims who had reportedly demanded a pea soup without ham and the dancehall for prayers had, in fact, arranged the modified menu a week in advance, and offered their prayers in the dance hall at the request of the owners, who wanted to free up the dining room for other patrons.

Drawing Lessons

As we have seen, many of the controversies involving Canadian Muslims are draped in double standards, hypocrisy, or confusion.

Most of the tensions surrounding Muslim religious practices are not exclusive to Muslims. People of other faiths face similar challenges in balancing their constitutional right to freedom of religion with other rights. Indeed, as Kymlicka notes, the tension

> typically involves white Christian groups – such as the evangelical Christian school in Quebec that seeks exemption from sex education, the evangelical Christian teachers' college in British Columbia that instructed teachers to view homosexuality as sin, the Catholic school board in Ontario that refused a gay student the right to attend his graduation, and so on (140–141).

It is also wrong to assume that Muslims are not adapting to Canadian values. They are – because they must, in that all must obey the rule of law, and there's no suggestion that they aren't, compared to the rest of the population. Polls also show that Muslims in Canada, the United States and across Europe share the same sense of belonging and hold the same values, hopes, and fears as their fellow-citizens (Adams, Esposito, Pew Global Attitudes Project). Canadian Muslims are also not making unreasonable demands, as the Bouchard-Taylor commission concluded.

Addressed to Quebecers, the commission's findings are relevant to all Canadians. "The right to freedom of religion includes the right to show it," said Taylor and Bouchard. They argued that the display of religion in public spaces advances the common good, by compelling all citizens to "get to know those of the Other, (rather) than deny or marginalize them" (120). Therefore, the hijab is fine in schools and elsewhere, as are the kippa, turban and kirpan. None violates anyone else's rights. The hijab is also fine in "sports competitions if it does not compromise the individual's safety." (The qualifier ought not to be used as a cover for bigotry in the name of safety.) Universities and schools should offer temporary space for prayers, while permanent spaces may be needed at "penitentiaries, hospitals, or airports, since those there are not free to visit a church" (178). Requests for such non-Christian religious holidays as Eid are legitimate. However, the duty of accommodation is not limitless. "A request may be rejected if it leads to what the jurists call 'undue hardship,' which can take different forms such as unreasonable cost, upsetting an organization's operation, infringing the rights of others, or prejudicing the maintenance of security and public order" (19). But, overall, the guiding principle should be: the more accommodation the better. Otherwise, "the rejection of certain requests risks producing the effect dreaded, i.e. encouraging certain individuals to withdraw from public institutions and cease to interact with the common culture . . . The most publicized cases involving Muslims all involved activities where they were participating or integrating into our society" (283).

These are sound Canadian principles, applicable to Muslims and non-Muslims alike. A democracy, especially as pluralistic as Canada's, could no more proscribe the hijab than ban a nun's habit, or a cardinal's skull cap or, for that matter, a bikini. As for the niqab, it may be imperative that a person's face be visible for security checks and in photographs on passports and driver's licences. But the state would need to pass a rational law in compliance with the *Charter* prescribing so, rather than leave the matter to the whims of Muslim-baiting politicians and media.

As Kymlicka writes,

> we must enforce the law, but we do not need to continuously test or provoke minorities . . . whether in the form of the Mohammed cartoon in Denmark or the veil law in France (2001), or, sadly, the anti-stoning law in Herouxville. This sort of provocation is self-defeating. If we tell immigrants that we don't trust them, and that we are monitoring their every word and reaction for hints of disloyalty or illiberalism, they will not feel that their political participation is welcomed and their political integration will be delayed, if not derailed entirely (153).

For their part, Muslims, too, ought to be mindful that they cannot expect exceptions from the rule of law. No aspect of sharia that may contravene Canadian law can be imported. Those who think they can practice polygamy in Canada, in the name of freedom of religion, are breaking Canadian law. Many Muslims often get bogged down in theological debates: What is the "right" interpretation of God's words in the Qur'an or of man-made laws of the sharia? As relevant as such debates are to Muslims, and of interest to non-Muslims, they are for the most part irrelevant for the purposes of public policy and legislative decision-making. A democratic state is not in the business of dictating which version of a religion should prevail. Conservative interpretations of Islam are as valid as conservative interpretations of Christianity, Judaism, or any other faith, so long as they do not contravene the law of the land.

A common mistake made by non-Muslims is to conflate Canadian Muslims with Muslims the world over. This is a by-product of a post-9/11 malaise: Laying collective guilt on all Muslims for the actions of a few. Law-abiding Muslims are no more responsible for 9/11 and the London subway bombings and other acts of terrorism than Japanese Canadians or Japanese Americans were for Pearl Harbor, or German Americans, German Canadians and German British were for Nazism. It is useful to recall what Anne Frank, hiding from the Nazis in Amsterdam during World War II, wrote in her famous diary, on May 22, 1944: "When a Christian does something wrong, it's his fault. When a Jew does, it's the fault of all Jews" (Frank, 299).

Yet it is often demanded of Canadian Muslims that they pronounce themselves on this or that Muslim atrocity somewhere in the world. Canadian Muslims live here in Canada, not there. This is not to deny that Muslim nations have a shameful record on many issues, including the treatment of women and minorities. But holding Canadian Muslims culpable for those sins would be like holding Serb Canadians responsible for the ethnic cleansing in Bosnia and Kosovo. It is also disingenuous to suggest that Canadian Muslims have less of a right to demand equality because non-Muslims in some Muslim lands are denied the most basic rights. During the *Maclean's* controversy, Rex Murphy, CBC-TV's commentator, made just such a sulphurous suggestion. He sneered that Canadian Muslims had the temerity to go to human rights commissions when "real human rights violations" were rampant across the Muslim world, especially in Saudi Arabia. Similar suggestions were heard, in a different context, by the Bouchard-Taylor commission, which rightly dismissed them as "deceitful" (Bouchard and Taylor, *Abridged*, 72).

Just as in an earlier era, Canadians had to battle anti-Catholicism and then, in another, anti-Semitism, and still must, this surely is the time to wrestle down anti-Islamism in our midst. That is our collective Canadian duty. Whatever damage post-9/11 paranoia may cause Muslims, it carries with it the greater danger of eroding our most fundamental democratic principles and damaging Canada's carefully crafted pluralistic polity.

Bearing the Name of the Prophet

SYED MOHAMED MEHDI

The Many Meanings of Mohamed (One Who is Praised)

In April 2004, I was flying to Chicago for a job interview at the American Philosophical Association's Midwestern meeting. Flying from Montreal, I had to clear US customs before boarding my plane. After showing my passport to an agent in line, I was sent into a separate room to be dealt with by a special officer. My passport was handed over to him in a see-through plastic bag. After making a few phone calls, he gestured for me to enter his office. I was a bit nervous. I wanted to get on my flight. He broke the ice with, "You have a very interesting name." When I politely thanked him for the compliment, he revised his statement: "You share your name with some very interesting people."

My great-grandfather on my paternal side was Mehdi Nawaz Jung. This was his noble title. His given name was Syed Mohamed Mehdi, a name that was passed on to me not because of, but despite, its religious grandeur. Mehdi Nawaz Jung was a generous, cosmopolitan, and forward-looking man. He left his origins in a traditional Muslim neighbourhood in the old city of Hyderabad and began to slowly develop the wilderness that was Banjara Hills. He wanted to build homes that were architecturally integrated with the unique rock formations indigenous to the area. Many relatives and friends, Muslim and Hindu, joined him there to form a kind of Shi'a colony. His idea was successful, more than he would have imagined or perhaps liked, as the area has developed into one of Hyderabad's commercial hubs. His original rock home is hidden on all sides by condominiums that have come up in the last decade. What was once called Road Number One in Banjara Hills is now called Mehdi Nawaz Jung Marg. Away from Hyderabad, Mehdi made a temporary home in Ahmedabad, where, as Governor of Gujarat in postindependence India, he hosted the Queen of England.

My mother's family came from a different side of town, from the humble enclaves of the Mahdavi community. Mahdavis are followers of the fifteenth-century religious leader Syed Muhammad of Jaunpur. They see him as the messiah, or Mehdi. As a result, Syed Mohamed Mehdi is a magical name among Mahdavis. I rediscovered this when I was in Chicago (the interview went well), and paid a cab driver with a credit card. Chicago has a large community of Mahdavis, so it was no surprise when the taxi driver smiled at the sight of my name on the card and asked if I, like him, came from Chanchalguda, Hyderabad.

There is an evidently Sufistic streak in the practices and beliefs of the Mahdavis. This may have nurtured my grandfather, who, after playing a leading role in organizing the peasant resistance in Telengana against the Muslim prince of Hyderabad, the Nizam (in whose employ Mehdi Nawaz Jung had toiled), became a professor of philosophy and an important figure in the Hyderabadi intellectual scene. He was also connected with the Progressive Writers Association, a loose and long-lived collective formed in the 1930s of leftist poets, writers, and even musicians, which had as one of its main organizers a man from Aligarh named Syed Mohammed Mehdi.

So I agreed with the immigration officer that I share my name with interesting people, though these were probably not the people he had in mind. On my way back to Canada, they allowed me back into the country of my birth only when I showed them the list of participants in the conference I had been attending, and they were satisfied to see that their names were not so interesting.

What's in a Name?

It had not always been like this. As a child, there were two things I really liked about my name. One, the proud fact that it was the most popular name in the world, more popular than John, as I liked to point out to my friends. Two, the even prouder fact that it was also the name of the heavyweight champion of the world. Countless people, when introduced to me, would ball their hands into fists, crouch down and say, "Hey it's Mohamed, like Muhammad Ali!" This was such a common occurrence that when I happened to meet the great fighter in a Chicago hotel as a young boy, a few years after his retirement, I felt like I was meeting an old friend. He was happy to hear my name, and responded with "Salaam Alaikum." It was Muhammad Ali who thus reminded me that my name was not a boxer's name so much as a Muslim name. I was, embarrassingly, too awed to respond with the requisite "Waaleykum Salaam."

I saw the power of my name once again many years later after a Baba Maal concert at Toronto's Roy Thomson Hall. A young Senegalese boy, maybe ten or twelve years old, was hawking tapes outside the auditorium. He asked my friends and me for our names. When he heard mine, he spontaneously leapt two feet into the air and landed in my arms. He hugged me tightly and exclaimed, "My Muslim brother!" I remember feeling guilty that I had not reciprocated the feeling of brotherhood. I feared that my name had provided him with a false sense of who I was, but was also proud of being a recognizable part of this universal community that knew no bounds of language or nationality. My parents had cultivated in me a careful distance from religious dogma and ritual; this had grown into a distrust of all organized forms of religious practice. And yet my name continued to assert that I was a Muslim, a brother or an enemy, depending on the perspective.

Bearing the Prophet's name has had an unmistakeable impact on my sense of who I am and of the world I live in. People's reactions to my name can be a barometer of the political climate I find myself in: the naivety of Canadians who had first heard "Mohamed" pronounced by Howard Cosell, the elation of the Senegalese tape-vendor at finding a brother, the fear felt by my mother in calling me by my name as we travelled by train in India in the early 1990's after the destruction of the Babri Masjid by the Hindu Right, led by the Rashtriya Swayamsevak Sangh, and the communal violence that ensued, and the extra special treatment I received at the American border. (There is also the sweet caution of my paternal grandmother, my Daadi, a devout Shi'a, who calls me Mo lest she should curse the Prophet's name when she is annoyed with me.) And while giving me a sense of what my name means in different political contexts, these kinds of incidents and countless others also give me a sense of how I am perceived and what I stand for to others, in those contexts.

The real issue is not, of course, that my name is specifically Mohamed, but, rather, that it is an obviously Muslim name. It is a unique identity marker. Unlike skin colour, for example, it is not always unchosen. Many converts to Islam take on a traditionally Muslim name, usually Arabic in origin. Even for those, like me, who were named at birth, it is always possible to change one's name. You can change your name officially, as some people in my family have in fact done. It can also be changed in a particular context, by introducing yourself, for example, as Mike. A new name can also be pulled out for specific occasions, such as when making a reservation at a restaurant for the "Maurice" party. But in many contexts, in school, at work, when travelling, when making business transactions, one's real name sticks, and with it, so does the identity of a Muslim.

The question of whether or not I am a Muslim, or in what sense I am a Muslim, did not seem so important to me at one time. Like many others, I held this to be a private matter and one that could be decided ultimately only on the basis of personal faith. Nowadays, I am not so sure that this is just a private matter concerning my religious beliefs. Discussions of Shari'a law and religious education in Ontario, of "reasonable accommodation" in Quebec, of citizenship and secularism in Europe, of the "problem" of Islam in the modern world generally, have placed the Muslim community at the centre of public debate that is ultimately concerned with the equal and just distribution of social and political rights. This has led me and many others to question where we are situated in this political landscape, whether or not our voices and lives should be thought of and projected as Muslim voices and lives, and to ask if there is room for us within the community of Muslims but outside the simplistic division into "moderates" and "extremists." Of course, the mere fact of one's name cannot decide this question, even if it identifies one as a Muslim. Just being perceived as a Muslim in some contexts is not enough to make one identify as a Muslim except in a very narrow sense. But it can serve as a powerful reminder that Islam is an important part of what makes me who I am, an aspect of my personal history that links me with many others with whom I share little else, but whose culture, household, expressions and values I can to at least a small extent understand from within.

It was this sense of a shared culture, rather than of identical beliefs or practices, that led the young Senegalese tape vendor to find in me a home away from home. In this case, religious identity was not simply the result of a personal choice, as it is often assumed to be. This suggests that in many cases being a Muslim is not a straightforward matter of freely adopting an internal faith, a belief in one God and Muhammad as his messenger, and expressing this through certain outward practices. Faith and religious belief are, by their very nature, private matters in a very literal sense: they cannot ultimately be verified by any external earthly entity. If you claim to hold a belief, I can contrast your claim with other things you have said or done, but I have no final test to decide whether or not you genuinely believe what you claim to.

There are, on the other hand, several widely recognized practices that are taken to be a sign of what one believes, and that come to play the role of criteria of religious belonging. Some of the outward signs of Islam, those that can be verified by others, that are most popularly referred to are avoidance of pork and alcohol, regular prayer, and fasting during Ramadan. Politically, these are perhaps less important than almsgiving and the injunction against usury. Nonetheless, the latter are not usually used as a test of Islamic identity. On other hand, someone who doesn't pray five times a day, or fast at the right times, or who drinks alcohol, is often considered not just a bad Muslim but, rather, not a Muslim at all. It has often been pointed out to me on such grounds that I am not a Muslim, both by Muslims and by others. Judgments of this kind, however, implicitly rank various aspects of Islamic practice in order of significance. There is, in most cases, no warrant for such a prioritization. In fact, when we hear calls for internal Islamic dialogue, at least part of what we should be discussing is what aspects of Islamic doctrine and practice are most important to us. If being a Muslim is treated merely as an all or nothing adherence to a specific set of practices, this would dramatically reduce both the ideological import of Islam as a culture and an ethical philosophy, and the number of people who are Muslims.

Another kind of outward sign of being Muslim is related to appearance, a certain style of beard and the hijab being the most prominent nowadays. The hijab is seen in the west as a religious symbol, a display of faith, and it is true that it is seen by both supporters and detractors as a symbol of religious identity, as a religious garment. But its status is a little different from a crucifix, for example. A hijab is a piece of cloth that a woman uses to cover her hair for the sake of modesty. This is Islamic only indirectly, because, according to many, Islam enjoins modesty on its followers and suggests the hijab as a means to modesty. A woman doesn't have to be a Muslim to wear a hijab, any more than a man must be a Muslim to grow a beard or be circumcised. Once again, if these aspects of physical appearance were to be the only signs of who is a Muslim, both the moral significance and the population of Muslims would sharply decline.

In recent years, one's name has also become an increasingly significant and widely recognized sign of being a Muslim in the west. In countries such as India or Sri Lanka, where Muslims are a traditional minority, this has long been the case. In Canada, ears have until recently been more sensitive to detecting names of different kinds of European origin. The increased recognizability of Muslim names is the product of recent policies of western governments, and I don't mean multicultural education. We hear the names of Arab, Pakistani, Irani, and Afghan leaders and militants in the news because of wars we are conducting. All kinds of agencies, professionals, and service agents have been taught, or have taught themselves, to screen and profile for Muslims, and the easiest way to do this is by learning to recognize Muslim names. Having an obviously Muslim name is a little like being dark-skinned: you can't pass.

In the end, none of these external signs bear any necessary relationship either with the sincerity of one's religious conviction or the depth of one's identification with other Muslims. Whether or not they are the result of a conscious choice, they are independent of each other, you can have one without the other, and all without any genuine faith. There is no easy and obvious test to decide who is a Muslim, and discussions of what it means to be a Muslim in our world should be open to a wide range of persons who are Muslims in perhaps very different senses.

Rediscovering Community

What does this mean for a person like me? My father, a staunch scientific rationalist, and my mother, the daughter of a Marxist organiser, did not name me Mohamed in order to be devout, but rather in honour of my great-grandfather. Both my parents shared their knowledge of the history and traditions of Islam with me, but not in order to make me into a good believer. In fact, if I had chosen to take the path of religious devotion I am sure I would have hidden it from my parents, at least at first. Nonetheless, my father occasionally took me to Majlis to mark the death of Imam Husain, and my mother showed me how to pray. My father also taught history at the Islamic school, mainly in order to counter some of the distortions he had begun to hear. Like my father and mother, and my grandparents before them, I remain attached to the progressive ideals that had been championed by the most prominent, creative, and politically engaged standard bearers of Muslim culture in twentieth century India and Pakistan. These were men and women, poets and writers, such as Faiz Ahmed Faiz, Maqdoom Mohiuddin, Saadat Hasan Manto, Ismat Chughtai who lived in an occasionally uneasy but respectful and active relationship with the broader Muslim community. My grandmother, Khadija Alam Khundmiri, was among the first, or perhaps the first, woman to seek municipal office in Hyderabad. She bravely fought for the economic rights of the women of Chanchalguda. When she was physically attacked, it was the women she represented who defended her by forming a human barrier. My grandmother died of cancer in 2000, not in a hospital but in a mosque, where our Murshad, or spiritual leader, prepared her for what lies beyond. Her story and the stories of thousands of women like her are not ever heard in discussions of Muslim society. And yet these are, without a doubt, Muslim women.

An important part of what makes these women Muslims is neither a mark worn externally nor a sincere faith in God and his prophet Muhammad, and it is also not their names. Rather, it is their self-identification with and immersion in a culture and broad ethical understanding that emerges from the Islamic societies that have produced such a diversity of individuals. For them, growing up in Muslim households and neighbourhoods, surrounded by Muslim stories, ideas, books, and traditions, Islam played a preeminently defining role in their lives. But when injustice was perpetuated in the name of Islam, they recognized that they must fight against it, just as they would fight against injustice originating from another source. In doing so, while they were open to external influences, they drew on central aspects of Muslim culture such as a strong egalitarianism, personal humility, a love of knowledge, the development of literary and intellectual skill, a powerful sense of community, and the example of countless predecessors in the struggle for justice. Their resistance, although it may often be oriented against an ingrained and powerful religious orthodoxy, is not oriented against Islam. However, their opposition to the more conservative and powerful religious leaders does not make them "moderate." They are radical believers in justice and equality, which are values central to Islam.

The current rhetoric about "moderate" Muslims is problematic in part because it places us on a scale of Muslimness with undefined units culminating in extremism, suggesting that the closer one is to the extreme end of the undefined but well-understood parameter, the closer one is to authenticity. The underlying assumptions are that to be a Muslim means being very devout, and that to be a devout Muslim and politically moderate is a difficult balancing act. This way of thinking is also problematic because it leaves progressive Muslims out of the picture altogether. We now have a situation in which Muslims with progressive ideals are not seen as Muslims and often do not consider themselves to be Muslims either. There are various reasons for this, but certainly one of them is a pervasive approach in the media and in official circles, which has filtered through to all of us, that has decided in strict terms what a Muslim must be for the sake of creating a political discourse about and with Muslims.

What is important at the end of the day is not who counts as a Muslim and who does not, not the tired art of classification, but rather the recognition that within the global community of Muslims, if it can be called that, there exists a rich variety of voices, stories, and traditions. We must attune our ears to this diversity if we are to achieve any kind of self-understanding. Rather than feel anxious about what it really means to be a Muslim, we must take joy in the fact that Islam can provide a way for people of different languages, nationalities, cultures, and personal beliefs to know and respect one another's struggles as humans.

Several years ago I felt uneasy with the identifications my name forced upon me. On the one hand I felt pigeonholed and on the other I felt inauthentic. I was proud of the historical connections of my name, but frustrated by being measured against a picture of what a Muslim is that I could not relate to. More recently, my name has led me to recognize that even though I may not carry the external signs associated with Islam, and even though my practices vary sharply with those enjoined by our religious leaders, I am, in part, a product of Muslim culture. And my name has provided me with a direct sense of what it has meant to be a Muslim in the west in the early twenty-first century, the age of "good" and "bad" Muslims, of sleeper cells, and of "reasonable accommodations." It has reminded me that the innocent victims in Iraq, Gujarat, or Afghanistan could have been me or members of my family. When my name is the basis for government profiling, when I cannot do simple things like open a bank account, rent an apartment, travel across borders, get visas without extra scrutiny, I am in the same position as millions of my brothers and sisters. In this context, my identification with progressive ideals has, perhaps ironically, led me to see that I should not fear the Muslim identity suggested by my name. During this same time, I have seen many who, as a result of their identification with Islam, have come to embrace a progressive political outlook, emphasizing the basis in Islamic beliefs for justice, equality, freedom, and pluralism. This convergence, although it hasn't been widely spoken of, is one of the few positive consequences for Muslims of the "war on terror" and its broader context. There is a potential for building on this in Canada, for slowly developing a broader sense of what it means to be a Muslim, grounded in those elements in Islam that have historically taught us about what it means to live well together respectfully, lovingly, as brothers and sisters. But this will only be possible as we begin fearlessly to explore the complexity of Muslim culture and the many meanings of "Mohamed."

Knowing the Universe in All its Conditions

ARIF BABUL

I am an astrophysicist, a physical cosmologist, and my work involves trying to understand how matter in the Universe, having emerged from the fires of the Big Bang in an exceedingly smooth and homogenous state nearly 14 billion years ago, managed to organize itself into something that resembles a network of matter filaments, bejeweled necklace strands if you will, strung with millions of galaxies and occasionally punctuated by massive swarms of up to a thousand bright galaxies held together by their mutual gravity, and all woven together in a glittering cosmic web draped across the incomprehensibly vast regions of space. And I am Muslim, a Shia Ismaili[1] Muslim to be specific. I would like to make clear at the outset that in using this label, I am not merely trying to situate myself in a historical and civilizational context; rather, I am referring to the faith itself and to its core spiritual and ethical vision. These two assertions, in juxtaposition, tend to evoke a broad range of responses, the most typical being discomfiture. Conditioned by the contemporary Western framing of the relationship between faith and science as being predominantly one of conflict, such a response is perfectly understandable. My audience – some professional colleagues and even some coreligionists – don't quite know what to think, how to react and more importantly, what to make of me. I will return to this issue of conflict in due course.

I am convinced that to be a scientist was bred in my bones. I have inherited my mother's facility with mathematics, her acute visual memory and my father's ability to absorb and assimilate information, be it medical, sociological, legal, historical, or commercial in character, and to be able to "see" the flow of an argument as well as its inherent patterns. Of course, with these traits, I could have pursued just about any profession – doctor, lawyer, engineer – but ever since I was a child, I have been fascinated by the natural world and intensely curious about how things work, about the law, order, and harmony of the physical world. I recall spending endless hours squatting by puddles that formed after tropical downpours in Tanzania, the country of my birth and childhood, and staring at the teeming life within. I also remember watching car mechanics take apart and put back engines and quizzing my mother about how rainbows form. I recall vividly standing on a beach in Dar es Salaam one late evening with my mother and her sister. I was six years old at the time. The Apollo 11 moon landing had just taken place and I was thoroughly enchanted by the whole idea of space and of distant planets. My mother and my aunt, having noticed my new fascination, decided to indulge me by pointing out the various constellations that they had learnt about during their tenure as Girl Guide leaders in their youth. I remember not paying attention. To this day, I am embarrassed to say that I would be hard pressed to identify more than four or five very well known constellations. Instead, the stars themselves had captured my attention. Why was one star in the constellation of Orion red while another, at the opposite corner, white? And why was there a faint "cloudlike" band that stretched across the sky each and every night that I checked, even though there had been no clouds in the sky earlier in the evening? And why did the stars set in the west, just like the sun?

Growing up, the notion that being a research scientist, that asking questions about the workings of the natural world would somehow put me in conflict with my faith was simply not part of my worldview. From very early on, my father encouraged me to listen in on the discussions that took place on a daily basis between himself and his close coterie of friends. These sessions typically touched upon a wide range of topics, ranging from philosophy and theology to sociology and psychology. I admit that I did not always take up the invitation. Playing tag, hide-and-seek, and badminton generally trumped listening to a group of adults. However, I did start to learn at an early age that thinking, asking questions, and even challenging established ideas through reasoned arguments was not a taboo. In fact, my father took great pains to teach me that this was part and parcel of the 1400-year-old intellectual heritage that the Ismailis are heir to. The resulting discourse sometimes led to my being introduced to the ideas expounded by Muslim scientists, philosophers, and poets such as Ibn al-Haytham, Nasir Khusraw, al-Tusi, Ibn Sina, Ibn Arabi, Rumi, Iqbal, etc. Many of these were not Ismailis themselves but their perspectives had much in common with Ismaili thought and in turn had either influenced its development or been influenced by it. During the course of these discussions, my father also introduced me to the discourses on the Shia interpretation of Islam by Imams Ali Ibn Talib and Jafar as-Sadiq, the first and the fifth (by Ismaili reckoning), respectively, in the line of hereditary Imams of the Shia Muslims, as well as to the speeches and writings of His Highness Prince Karim Aga Khan, the present and the forty-ninth Imam of the Shia Ismaili Muslims in direct lineal descent from Prophet Muhammad, as well as those of his predecessor, Sir Sultan Muhammad Shah Aga Khan III.

Today, I understand that the reason why I am at ease with my scientist self and my Muslim self existing as an entangled whole, why I don't find it necessary to segregate these two aspects of my being into two distinct and separate compartments, is directly the consequence of my having been brought up in such a milieu. I can certainly imagine that a very different path may well have triggered an internal crisis or engendered a very different response. For example, a number of verses in the Qur'an, if taken literally, evoke imagery that is more compatible with the accepted geocentric cosmology of the time than the contemporary heliocentric one, a description that was unproblematic until Galileo and Kepler firmly established that the earth orbited the sun rather than vice versa in the early 1600s. Reading into these verses a conflict between science and faith depends entirely on how one chooses to engage with the Qur'anic text. To be fair, most Muslims, much less those who belong to paths within Islam that have historically advocated an intellectual or an esoteric engagement with the Qur'an, tend to steer away from simple literalism. Instead, at the popular level at least, "creative literalism," along the lines popularized by M Bucaille,[2] is the fashion of the day, as evidenced by the mass appeal of the countless websites advocating this view.

In brief, this viewpoint argues that all contemporary scientific facts and concepts can be found within the Qur'anic text. In order to make this happen, however, the imagery in the Qur'an needs to be stretched, and then some. One example of this is a particularly popular email that attempts to validate the Qur'an by drawing attention to a "colour" image of the Cat's Eye Nebula constructed (I use this word deliberately) from observations by the Hubble Space Telescope. The text attached to the email argues that the following verses foretold this cosmic phenomenon's existence: "When the sky disintegrates, and turns rose-coloured like paint. Which of your Lord's marvels can you deny?"[3] The Hubble image circulated with the text does indeed look like a "rose-coloured" painting (there are other Hubble images of the same nebula with very different colour schemes), but it hardly gives the impression of the sky "disintegrating." A nebula, a celestial smudge really, occupies a patch of the sky much smaller than that covered by a dime held at arm's length and is impossible to see with the naked eye. Seen through the eyepiece of a telescope, it has a fuzzy blue-green (not red) appearance. The Hubble image in question is a false-colour composite, a stylized rendition if you will, in which the colours do not necessarily correspond to those that the human eye perceives but rather, to the visual representation of three sets of observations that were fine-tuned to isolate emissions from hydrogen, oxygen and nitrogen atoms. Setting all this aside, an examination of the two verses in their proper context clearly shows that the phrase "When the sky disintegrates . . ." refers to the arrival of the Day of Reckoning.

As a way of engaging with the Qur'an, I find this approach no less problematic than literalism. After all, if ideas such as the Big Bang are recorded explicitly in the Qur'an, why didn't any one notice prior to the 1930s, or to put it more bluntly, why did it take a non-Muslim to discover it? Moreover, science is constantly revising itself. Scientific ideas are always at risk of being altered to give better approximations to physical reality, or even discarded if nature provides evidence to the contrary. I can't help but wonder what textual sleight-of-hand the proponents of this particular approach will engage in, if after decades of emphatically claiming that the Qur'an predicted the Big Bang, this particular model is replaced by something altogether different. I find the popularity of this trend worrisome. It suggests that, at the popular level at least, Muslims are becoming disconnected with their own rich historical tradition of intellectual engagement with the Qur'an, and consequently there is a rising level of insecurity about how to respond to science. I worry that "creative literalism" does a tremendous disservice to the rich body of work that comprises Islamic thought, and risks tarring Muslims, and by extension Islam, as lacking intellectual depth. I also worry that within Muslim societies, "creative literalism" is tilling the ground for an unnecessary future conflict.

In contrast to literalism or even "creative literalism," the perspective that I have grown up with is that the Divine Message speaks primarily to humanity's relationship with the Divine, offering a spiritual and ethical outlook aimed at ennobling human existence, giving it meaning and purpose, and it does this through the use of metaphors and allegories. It is also the running thread through the detailed exposition of the proper code of conduct that the nascent Muslim community was meant to live by. The challenge is for Muslim societies, at any time and in any geographical and cultural setting, to draw out this thread rather than fixate on the literal. Implicit in this understanding is the notion that the expressed form of the Divine message, the specificity of the code of conduct as well as the basis and the structure of the language and the metaphors, must be understood in the context of the womb of history and culture, within which it took form, that the Revelation ought to be seen as a Dialogue framed by the historical events and experiences of the Prophet, his companions and the nascent community of believers at the time. To the extent that the Discourse refers to the physical universe that humans inhabit, it does so through spatial, temporal and even conceptual reference points rooted in specific understandings and experiences of the Arabs to whom the Prophet was speaking. They are not framed as "scientific propositions" about how the physical world works. And contrary to contemporary efforts to turn them into such *a posteriori*, most schools of thought within Islam, of which the Ismaili tariqah (path) is one, have never understood them as such, interpreting them instead as metaphors speaking to issues central to humanity, human existence and the moral shape that that existence ought to take. It is because of this that the shifting of the cosmic centre from the earth to the sun caused little or no spiritual turmoil within much of the Islamic world. The verses in question were generally interpreted as referring to humanity's central position within creation in a spiritual and metaphysical sense, and of its capacity, having been bestowed by the Divine gift of the intellect in its broadest sense – rational, spiritual, emotional, moral, etc. – to get to know the Mystery of the Divine. This had not changed.

The story of Adam and Eve is a case in point. Informed by the acrimonious polemics of the Biblical literalists as well as the fervently antireligious ideologues within the scientific community, which followed Charles Darwin's and Alfred Russell Wallace's hypothesis that all organisms on earth, humanity included, have descended with modifications from a common ancestor, this story has come to epitomize the presumed conflict between science and faith in the Western popular imagination. Today, on the strength of considerable accumulated evidence, biologists accept evolution as a fact, much like gravity is a fact, and the research is focused mostly on elucidating the mechanisms that underlie biological evolution. Interestingly, it is not only the literalists that are troubled by evolution. Even the Roman Catholic Church, which does not necessarily advocate the literal reading of the Bible, has difficulty with some of its aspects. As discussed by Richard C Lewontin, in a highly recommended essay titled "The Wars over Evolution,"[4] the Church's current position – as outlined by Cardinal Christoph Schonborn in a *New York Times* article – accepts the "historical fact that life has evolved" and that "human and other organisms have a common ancestry and, by implication, that the species on earth today have evolved over a long period from other species no longer extant." What the Church has trouble with is the idea that the emergence of humans as a species is an outcome of "pure chance and necessity." As Lewontin explains:

> For if evolution is only the consequence of random mutations, none of which needs to have occurred, and if the subsequent fate of those mutations is subject only to the relative ability of their carriers to reproduce and to survive catastrophes of the environment that eliminate species and make

room for new ones, then rational beings capable of moral choices might never have come into existence. But without such beings, the concept of Redemption is unintelligible. Christianity demands, at the very least, the inevitable emergence of creatures capable of sin. Without a history of human sin, there is no Christ.

I know that many Muslims are troubled by the idea of "chance and necessity" but this has little to do with the concept of Original Sin perpetrated by the Biblical Adam and Eve, and the resultant "fall of man" that is at the heart of the Roman Catholic concept of Redemption. Such concepts are not part of the Islamic version of the story. Moreover, Muslim thinkers and mystics, like Ibn Arabi, were more inclined to focus on its allegorical nature. It is of no importance that in this story, Adam is fashioned out of clay, at least not in the literal sense. The idea of gods fashioning human beings (and sometimes other animals as well) out of clay or mud is a particularly common motif in creation myths dating back to the very first human civilizations that sprang up on the banks of the Nile, the Tigris/Euphrates, and the Yangtze. In the Qur'anic context, this well-known story offers an apt setting for situating mankind intellectually, morally, and spiritually within creation. The focus of the story is on the Divine gift of the intellect. It is this faculty that sets humanity apart from the rest of creation, which offers human beings the promise of being able to rise above their mundane origins and its attendant impulses. It is this faculty through which mankind becomes capable of knowing the "names of all things." It is important to note that "intellect" as used here does not refer merely to the faculty that facilitates knowing in the rational sense. Rather, "knowing" extends to spiritual, moral, and emotional sensitivity as well. And having been given the ability to know, humanity has no excuse for not aspiring to become "good" in the Aristotelian sense. The story further acknowledges that humans are fallible but also capable of recognizing their mistakes and making amends if given appropriate guidance. The story concludes not with humankind shouldered with sin but rather with the understanding that guidance will always be available, and that the legacy of the prophets, of Prophet Muhammad (and of the Imams, within the Shia tradition) is to be regarded as evidence of Divine Mercy. Framed in this fashion, the story of the Creation takes on a very different meaning.

The approach outlined above is neither a contemporary phenomenon nor is it unique to the Ismailis. Both Shia and Sunni scholars have historically subscribed to it. In discussing this very idea at a public lecture[5] delivered at the University of Victoria in June 2001, Ebrahim Moosa,[6] presently a professor of Islamic Studies at Duke University and a 2005 Carnegie Scholar, drew upon a series of verses from the Qur'an in support of his thesis: "Give good tidings to those of my servants who listen to the Word and follow the best part of it. Those are the people who God has guided and those are the people of insight."[7] He argued that today's Muslims are expected, required in fact, to struggle, to expend time and intellectual labour to identify between what is "better" and "best," to draw out from the historically contingent and culturally specific that which is universal and eternal, so that they can then manifest these ideals in their own lives and within their societies.

As the following quote from a lecture delivered by the Aga Khan at the opening session of a workshop titled "Word of God, Art of Man: The Qur'an and its Creative Expression," held in London, in October 2003, acknowledges, this approach is bound to give rise to a plurality of interpretations:

> . . . the Qur'an-e-Sharif, rich in parable and allegory, metaphor and symbol, has been an inexhaustible well-spring of inspiration, lending itself to a wide spectrum of interpretations. This freedom of interpretation is a generosity which the Qur'an confers upon all believers, uniting them in the conviction that All-Merciful Allah will forgive them if they err in their sincere attempts to understand His word. Happily, as a result, the Holy Book continues to guide and illuminate the thought and conduct of Muslims belonging to different communities of interpretation and spiritual affiliation, from century to century, in diverse cultural environments.[8]

Clearly, a plurality of interpretations is not seen as problematic. Rather, it is viewed as an outcome that is both acknowledged and embraced by the Qur'an itself as indicated by verses such as "those who strive in Our path, We will open up for them multiple ways" (9:20). Varying interpretations, as long as they represent a genuine search for understanding and meaning, are to be viewed as a positive. Drawing together these various threads within the Qur'an, Ebrahim Moosa argued in his lecture that even the very first message that Prophet Muhammad received, the imperative *iqra'* (recite!) can be read as an affirmation of this idea:

> One interpretation of "recite" is that Muhammad must tell, and retell the story of humanity. He must reexamine life around him and describe it with a particular urgency in his voice for the renewal of humanity ... to "recite" the story, not as a series of random arbitrary events, but as a search to understand the ultimate meaning found in the narrative that was unfolding around [him] and his community in the seventh-century Arabian peninsula. God ... wants everyone to retell, "recite," the story. From the beginning of the first [revelation], ... there is a requirement to tell and retell the story within the context of history.[9]

And this act of "retelling" demands an active engagement. Indeed in most schools within Islam, and especially in the Shia tradition, the human intellect is recognized as a precious Divine gift, to be used rather than stifled. Muslims are enjoined to reflect upon the Divine signs, whether they are found in the Qur'an or elsewhere, "standing, sitting and lying down on their sides."[10]

To understand nature itself, the Qur'an calls upon Muslims to study the physical world directly. My own reading is that the phrasing is even stronger. Muslims are directed or challenged to study nature in order to discover the mechanisms governing physical phenomena and to harness them for the benefit of humanity. Beyond this utilitarian agenda, the Qur'an also speaks of the Universe as pregnant with signs evoking the Divine. These verses sketch out a Universe in which the very order, exactitude and harmony of the natural world points to a real "something" of which we are part of but which also transcends us. I must admit that I find myself particularly drawn to these latter ideas; they resonate deeply with my theoretical physicist's view of the Universe. Inspired by such verses, Ismailis have historically emphasized the complementarity between knowledge acquired through reason, revelation, inspiration, and experience, the idea being that all provide different perspectives into the mystery of God. The quote "My profession is to be forever journeying, to travel about the Universe so that I may know all its conditions," which provided the title to this essay, and has been attributed to Ibn Sina, a brilliant tenth- and eleventh-century physician, philosopher, mathematician, and astronomer, speaks to this. Indeed, it has been argued that the Qur'anic verses that speak collectively to these notions provided the impetus for the emergence of the culture of unhindered scientific enquiry in early and medieval Muslim societies that led to the establishment of the first universities in the modern sense, as well as institutes and observatories dedicated to scientific and philosophical enquiry. These verses are also believed to have inspired scientific luminaries, such as the physicist Ibn al-Haytham and the astronomer al-Tusi, whose studies established some of the foundational ideas on which the edifice of contemporary science rests.

When I speak to my professional colleagues about their perspective on science and faith, those who see the two as conflicting schools of thought explain their position by noting that whenever religious texts "trespass" into the domain of science by trying to explain aspects of the natural world, it is inevitably incorrect and hence, in constant tension with science. This argument, however, is only effective against those who advocate a literalist approach to such texts; a more nuanced approach to the text along the lines adopted by Muslim intellectuals over the centuries vitiates this particular critique. Of course, such an approach is by no means unique to Islam. For example, both Augustine of Hippo and Thomas Aquinas, two philosopher-theologians who profoundly influenced Western Christian thought, as well as Moses Maimonides, whose works are regarded as a cornerstone of Jewish thought, engaged with the Biblical text very differently compared to today's literalists. Indeed, over the centuries, the intellectual discourse within Christianity about the relationship between faith and science parallels that in Islam. Without downplaying the occasional tension between science and religious dogma of the time, the idea of the two being in a perpetual state of conflict only entered into the popular imagination of the Western world in the closing decades of the nineteenth century. This period witnessed an especially intense level of antagonism between the Church, both the Roman Catholic Church as well as the Church of England, and the scientific community of the time. The reasons for this antagonism are varied and far more involved than the simplistic explanations typically bandied about.

In England, where much of the drama unfolded, the antagonism can partly be attributed to undercurrents already present in the broader society at the time, including the rise of evangelicalism and literalism within the Church of England. (In this respect, the parallel with the present-day evolution of Muslim societies, especially if one notes that literalism and creative literalism are close cousins, is quite troubling.) It was in this milieu that the "conflict thesis" emerged, propelled into popularity by its chief proponents, John William Draper and Andrew Dickson White. The key thesis put forth by Draper and White was that the historical record of the relationship between religion (which at the time meant "Christianity" but was subsequently generalized to encompass all religions) and science is best described as "a narrative of the conflict of two contending powers, the expansive force of the human intellect on one side, and the compression arising from traditionary faith and human interests on the other."[11] The idea of a perpetual conflict captured public imagination and continues to command popular appeal largely because of the vitriolic challenge to the teaching of the theory of evolution as part of science education in public schools by creationists – that is, those who take the Book of Genesis's description of the "origin of man" as literal truth. Today, however, most historians of science dismiss the premises underlying the "conflict thesis" as inaccurate, selective, and at best a gross simplification. For example, the most oft-quoted proof of the "conflict hypothesis," the persecution of Galileo by the Roman Catholic Church ignores the fact that many of Galileo's powerful patrons and supporters were members of the clergy and that Galileo's "persecution" owes much to human foibles, personality clashes, and political maneuvering. In short, the true state of affairs is much more complicated.

The actual interplay between science and religion has been shown to be much more complex, spanning the full spectrum from discord to concord depending on, among other factors, the specific theological and philosophical beliefs framing the discussion. A number of key scientific developments, like the idea of the Big Bang, are grounded in religious imagery and concepts. Moreover a number of scientists, Newton, Einstein, and Planck among them – the latter being one of the most influential physicists of the twentieth century as well as the originator of the quantum theory, which along with Einstein's theory of relativity, is a cornerstone of modern physics – were deeply spiritual in their outlook. In his 1937 lecture "Religion and Naturwissenschaft," Planck held that God (though not necessarily a personal God) is everywhere present, and "the holiness of the unintelligible Godhead is conveyed by the holiness of symbols."[12] Many of today's scientists who oppose religion dismiss this particular aspect of these scientists' character as idiosyncratic in spite of the fact that this perspective shaped their scientific outlook and inspired their science. And while contemporary myth holds that Kepler's mathematical laws governing planetary motion excludes the notion of an involved deity, neither Kepler nor Newton interpreted it as such. As noted by science writer and commentator M Wertheim:

> Kepler saw the world as the material embodiment of mathematical forms present within God before the act of creation. "Why waste words?" he wrote, "Geometry existed before the Creation, is co-eternal with the mind of God . . . geometry provided God with a model for the Creation." Thus, "where matter is, there is geometry." Because he believed that the world was a reflection of God, who was a perfect being, according to Kepler it must necessarily be a perfect world, and therefore the manifestation of sublime geometric principles. "It is absolutely necessary that the work of such a perfect creator should be of the greatest beauty."[13]

And indeed, mathematics or more precisely, mathematics that

contains inherent symmetries – not only physical symmetries of the kind we see in the construction of the Taj Mahal or in a snowflake, but also more abstract forms of symmetries – appears to have within it the power to take seemingly disparate physical phenomena, distill them down to their essence and bind them all into an ever-growing fold of unity. The laws that govern the natural world at the most fundamental level are not just a haphazard collection of rules; rather, they all appear to flow from a single unifying principle, and the fundamental particles that comprise matter, ordinary or otherwise, emerge "naturally as nearly ideal embodiments of the intricate, abstract symmetry principles"[14] within the mathematical forms of the theories of fundamental interactions.

This "order and harmony" in nature has been (and continues to be) a source of both enthrallment and considerable mystification among physical scientists, especially theorists. Why nature has a mathematical character to it is something that we simply do not understand. In Einstein's words: "The most incomprehensible thing about the Universe is that it is comprehensible."[15] Yet, we accept it as an article of faith, and this faith has served us well over the years. There are countless examples in the annals of physics where the search for beauty, elegance, and symmetry within the mathematical forms of the physical laws has led to discoveries of new phenomena and new forms of matter. Still, it is an article of faith. Eugene Wigner, physicist and Nobel laureate, in writing about the "unreasonable effectiveness of mathematics in natural sciences," concluded that

> The miracle of the appropriateness of the language of mathematics for the formulation of laws of physics is a wonderful gift, which we neither understand nor deserve. We should be grateful for it and hope that it will remain valid in future research and that it will extend, for better or worse, to our pleasure, even though perhaps to our bafflement, to wide branches of learning.[16]

And for many physicists – myself included – this and other similar aspects of our work inherently imply that the physical Universe is not merely a human construct, nor are our theories merely ways of relating groups of measurements. Rather, there exists an inherent order and harmony underlying the physical Universe and this is seen as indicating the existence of something "real" that transcends the physical. Our physical theories represent human efforts to glimpse at this reality, always approximate and always limited but improving with every successive refinement. And it would appear that the expressive language of this reality – in so far as the physical world is concerned – is mathematics: Referring to this power of mathematics, Einstein – in a lecture at the University of Oxford – said:

> I am convinced that we can discover by means of purely mathematical constructions . . . the key to understanding of natural phenomena. Experience may suggest the appropriate mathematical concepts, but they most certainly cannot be deduced from it . . . The creative principle lies in mathematics. In a sense, therefore, I hold it true that pure thought can grasp reality, as the ancients dreamed.[17]

It was to the process of uncovering these fundamental harmonies in nature that Einstein, when asked why he did what he did, responded "I'm not interested in this or that phenomenon, in the spectrum of this or that element. I want to know [God's] thoughts; the rest are details."[18] Of course, I should make clear that this power of mathematics is at present most powerfully manifest on the most fundamental stratum of the physical world. As phenomena become more and more complex, the power of our current mathematics fades. However, acknowledging the present-day limitations does not in any way take away from the question of why mathematics works in the very first place. And in fact, the very aesthetic of beauty – in the form of symmetry, for example – still continues to inform research in theoretical physics today. The holy grail of modern physics is to discover the single unifying principle that contains within it, in the form of symmetries for example, the full gamut of physical phenomena that animate the Universe – multiplicity emerging out of Unity as it reflects within itself. I can't help but be struck by the parallels in poetic symbolism of this thought with those of Muslim mystics over the ages.

If my descriptions above evoke the image of human beings – scientists – standing back, detached, this is because science as a communal or collective activity actively strives for such objectivity. The fantastic success of science is the direct result of this. Individual scientists, however, are very human, subject to very human impulses born of passion and prejudice, and in common with artists, musicians and poets, subject to powerful, transformative moments of what I can only describe as "inspiration." Kepler, for example, writes of being moved to a state of "unutterable rapture" at the unfolding of what he called the "divine spectacle of the heavenly harmony."[19] I know of what he speaks. I too have experienced such moments. For example, I remember well one such incident. I had just returned home – to prepare for my wedding – after my first year at Princeton. I was working on a conceptually challenging research program with Bohdan Paczynski, a faculty member in the Department of Astrophysical Sciences at Princeton. I was sitting at the dining table in a puddle of papers with equations scribbled all over, surrounded by the hubbub of family members who were playing, talking, laughing, and busy with chores. I had been working at this problem for weeks and I was beyond frustration. I remember suddenly being transported away, away from the sights and sounds of my immediate surroundings, and I could "feel" the solution. I use the word "feel" deliberately for I know of no other way of describing it. For a few moments, there was no "I," no "it." I was overcome with awe and of "littleness," intuitively aware of, almost touching, reality. I realize that the words are not coming out right. I realize that I am not doing justice to the experience. And I realize that all this probably sounds insane. But there it is. I have since spoken to many of my artist and poet friends and found that they too – on rare occasions – experience "this touching of reality." And until a few weeks ago, the only scientist that I knew of who had spoke of such things was Einstein:

> The most beautiful experience we can have is the mysterious. It is the fundamental emotion that stands at the cradle of true art and true science. Whoever does not know it and can no longer wonder, no longer marvel, is as good as dead, and his

eyes are dimmed. It was the experience of mystery – even if mixed with fear – that engendered religion. A knowledge of the existence of something we cannot penetrate, our perceptions of the profoundest reason and the most radiant beauty, which only in their most primitive forms are accessible to our minds: it is this knowledge and this emotion that constitute true religiosity. In this sense, and only this sense, I am a deeply religious man.[20]

While I was writing this paper, a friend suggested that I read an essay titled "A Sense of the Mysterious"[21] by physicist, novelist and essayist Alan Lightman. Having now read the essay, I am simply astonished – taken aback, in fact – at the similarities between Lightman's experience while growing up and my own, especially given the dissimilarity of the milieus in which we grew up. In his essay, Lightman writes of his "creative moment." And again, the parallel is surreal. Lightman's prose is beautiful and he does the experience much more justice than I have in a few sentences above.

I had experienced such moments before and have experienced it several times since, sometimes in the context of physics and sometimes under very different circumstances. And ever since the very first time, I have been struggling to make sense of it. In this, I have found the description of such experiences by contemporary philosopher Charles Taylor,

> We all see our lives and/or the space wherein we live our lives, as having a certain moral/spiritual shape. Somewhere, in some activity, or condition, lies a fullness, a richness; that is, in that place (activity or condition), life is fuller, richer, deeper, more worthwhile ... more what it should be ... We often experience it as deeply moving, as inspiring. Perhaps this sense of fullness is something we catch a glimpse of from afar off; we have the powerful intuition of what fullness would be, were we to be in that condition ... or able to act on that level, of integrity or generosity or abandonment or self-forgetfulness. But sometimes there will be moments of experienced fullness, of joy and fulfillment, where we feel

ourselves there ... [or there] may be moments when ordinary reality is "abolished" and something terrifyingly *other* shines through.[22]

and the words of the former Imam of the Ismailis, Aga Khan III, most illuminating:

> All those sunrises and sunsets – all the intricate miracle of sky colour, from dawn to dusk ... As a very rich man treasures the possessions of some unique picture, so a man should treasure and exult in the possession – his individual possession – of the sights of this unique world. Those glories are his from dawn to dusk, and then – and then comes night – "a night of stars" ... I look up at night and I know – I *know* the glory of the stars. It is then that the stars speak to us – and the sense of that mystery is in our blood.[23]

But if truth be told, I am still struggling to know and to know what it means to know. There is much more that can be said, much more that can be discussed. But perhaps this is a good place to pause.

Raising Muslim Children in a Diverse World

RUKHSANA KHAN

In our home there was always one authority that everyone, even the parents, were accountable to. Even before we had children, my husband and I decided to solve any differences by turning back to God, and the laws inscribed in the Qur'an and the hadith. This attitude has been the glue that has held us together for almost thirty years, and more so, has given our children recourse to take us to task on occasion.

It's quite difficult to raise religious children in the face of all the temptations in this society that can lure one away from a devout path. This is particularly challenging when as a parent you deliberately decide to send them to public schools. By raising the bar high, expecting them to do well not only in academics but also in matters of faith, I must say that we helped them succeed.

The stereotype of "religiously indoctrinated" children is that they are meek and submissive with low self-esteem. My experience though, has been quite the opposite. The key lies in the children's ability to internalize the religious values and accompanying restrictions, to own them as their personal values, so that when temptations arise and they have the strength to resist, that act of resistance also creates a sense of accomplishment and pride in their ability to stick to their principles.

With all the emphasis put on building self-esteem in children as a tool to enable them to make good choices later on in life, it is my belief that developing self-restraint and good moral values (as opposed to showering children with empty praise) is ultimately what develops a sense of healthy self-esteem in children. When children develop the strength to do what is right, even when it is not expedient, they feel good about the sacrifice they made and, consequently, they feel good about themselves.

Giving children standards to aspire to like integrity, honesty, and fairness to others is not what puts excess pressure on them. What puts pressure on them is expecting them to deal with factors beyond their control. For example, expecting them to be the most valuable player (MVP) on their softball team or the winner of the science fair project is an unreasonable load to carry. These are unrealistic expectations on the part of parents that can put harmful pressure on children because often such matters come down to factors beyond the child's control. To be the MVP doesn't take into consideration the abilities and circumstances of other children. One year the competition might be scant, while the following year children may face tremendous competition. Similarly, expecting them to win the science fair project doesn't take into consideration the excellent work other children might have done. Ultimately they need to learn to compete with themselves, that is, to do the best that they are capable of, to take pride in that accomplishment and at the same time appreciate the efforts of others. Emphasis should be put on whether a child is learning from the experience, learning teamwork and sportsmanship. We all know that for some parents their children exist to live out the frustrated dreams of their own childhood.

In our house, marks were considered only one factor that reflected how well the child had learned the curriculum. If a child had failed a test, but then gone back and learned from his or her mistakes, realized where they'd gone wrong and then corrected it, then that was considered a successful learning experience.

Early on we made a conscious choice to send our children to public schools because we wanted our children to learn to get along with all kinds of people, not just Muslims. They would eventually be integrated into general society and they would have to be able to maintain their beliefs while doing so. And what better way than to be immersed at a young age?

It wasn't easy. Not for them and not for us. So many times I had to explain to them why we don't do Halloween or Christmas, why we don't believe in Santa Claus and I had to explain to them that they still needed to be respectful of those who did. It was in grade two that one of the teachers got very frustrated with me. I had asked that my children not be given Halloween or Christmas activities to do. I didn't want them making ghosts and tree decorations or colouring in pictures of Santa Claus, and so I asked that they please be excluded from these activities. The teacher said it was difficult to exclude them all the time. (This was before teachers and the school board were more accommodating of religious differences.) And if I wanted them to be removed from all this stuff why hadn't I sent them to the Islamic school down the road? I told her that I had gone through the public school system myself and I really believe in the idea of all kids going to a common school, learning to get along with one another. And she said, "But there are so many times you have to say 'no.'"

At that point I looked at her blankly. Of course my kids would have to say no. How would they ever learn to say no to the pressures that would come later, as teenagers, if they didn't start out practising when they were young? If they couldn't get comfortable with who they were and what they stood for when they were in grade two and the temptations were few (just a few Halloween treats and Christmas candies), how would they ever survive the pressures of drugs and conformity and dating when they were teens? I tried to explain to her that this was all training. But from her blank stare I could tell that she was the one who couldn't get it.

Having gone through the public system myself I knew very well all the temptations that lurk out there. Each generation seems to think they're the ones who've discovered sin and decadence. And while the level of promiscuity among teens has gotten worse over the years and there are a wider range of drugs for them to get addicted to, the fact is that all these temptations were just as available when I was growing up. Sometimes I wonder what prevented me from indulging. It wasn't my parents. I could have gotten away with such behaviour without them knowing. But my father had instilled in us at an early age not only to fear him, but to fear God.

My father, being quite the storyteller, told us a story of a Muslim teacher who had long ago tested his students by asking them to take a chicken and find a place where no one could see them and then slaughter it and bring it back. All the students but one quickly returned. Finally, the last student arrived still with the chicken alive.

The teacher questioned him about it and the student said that he hadn't been able to find a place where God was not watching him. This idea was reinforced in me and my siblings as we grew up. Many times my parents warned me that I might be able to fool them but I couldn't fool God or myself. And I, in turn, told this story to my own children to remind them to be conscious of God.

Temptation and sin are tests and trials for us. They are choices we can make or avoid. That's what this whole life comes down to. We have a choice of acting upon what we know is right and continuing to develop our characters towards excellence or indulging in what we know is wrong for which we will eventually pay a moral price. Completely sheltering children from temptations is not only unrealistic but unproductive. Saying no to temptations and teaching them to say no to temptations really can make them stronger in the end.

The problem that some parents get into is when they say no they offer no explanations as to why. In order to be convincing, parents must work through all of the reasons why they maintain their religious principles, and then over time impart these philosophies to their children. Children have to see that parents have encountered and understand the pressures they are up against, and that there are good reasons for rejecting them.

Saying-no moments, become teachable moments. Parents shouldn't let them rush by without exploiting them. Of course, children being who they are will need repeated explanation. You will need to explain in a dozen different ways, reinforcing the concepts of religious limits over and over again. And again, being children, they will test those limits over and over again. Consistency is the key, and it is important to set the limits within a sort of safety zone. Perhaps this is best achieved by setting the prohibitions with some wiggle room built in for them to make mistakes. For example, when I was growing up, not only were we not allowed sexual freedom, we were not allowed to go to school dances, to date, and generally, to be in any situation that could even remotely lead to temptation.

Having placed these restrictions on us, my parents would however help us out in other ways to have a social life. They would take us to the mosque to socialize and study with other Muslims and they would drop us off and pick us up from Islamic camps and conferences. And when my turn came, I also provided alternative activities to school dances and dating. I would drive my own daughters to socialize with friends at the mosque and the mall.

You can also use talk shows to make your point. Sometimes I'd leave on an episode of Oprah about teen pregnancy even when my children, prepubescent at the time, were around, and I'd sit back and watch them watch the show. The conclusions they came to were better than any lecture I could have given them on the pitfalls of being sexually active at a young age. They felt these girls were ruining their lives engaging in promiscuity, not valuing themselves. I didn't have to say a thing except when they asked for my input and I agreed with them.

The key to getting children to listen to these limits is by example. They must see that you consistently apply these limits to your own life as well. That you are not asking them to do something that you are not doing yourself, in effect, that you practice what you preach. If you tell children not to lie, they should see that you do not lie yourself. If you tell children to deal honestly, they can't see you stealing towels from a hotel or playing with the odometer of your vehicle so it fetches a better price. If you tell your children to pray five times a day they must see you doing so, even when it is inconvenient. When you are out and about and prayer time comes, they must see you make a Herculean effort to find a place to pray. They must see you getting agitated when prayer time is getting late. In effect they must see you take the timeliness of your prayer as an appointment with God as seriously as you would take a job interview.

And when you slip up and they call you on it, you must not try to justify your actions. You must swallow your pride, admit your mistake, and show them that you plan to do better next time and that we all slip up now and then – no one is perfect.

These are ways to reinforce religious teachings in children, but at the same time, they need to learn tolerance of others and the best way to learn tolerance is to make sure you do things as a family outside your own cultural sphere. My parents liked to travel. My father figured a vacation where we drove across Canada was basically the cost of gas since we still had to buy food and we could sleep in the van. And so we drove right across this amazing continent. Back when there were so few traveling immigrants, we stopped to see the sights and sometimes we were stared at almost as much as the tourist attractions. And in the every day practise of common politeness in dealing with people from all over, we learned how to fit in, how to belong in this adopted country of ours.

With my own children we made sure to take them away from the city as often as we could. We went camping and made short trips across Northern Ontario. And we took them on longer trips to places like Nova Scotia and Boston. They learned canoeing and archery, rock-climbing and swimming. We took advantage of some of the cultural events in Toronto, and visited Caravan and umpteen events at Harbourfront. We took them to museums and historical venues like Black Creek Pioneer Village where they could appreciate the history of this country. And during all those family outings, we as parents tried our best to set examples for courteous, friendly, and tolerant behaviour. When our children made xenophobic remarks, as children are wont to do, they were quickly taken to task and reminded that we would not appreciate such comments directed at ourselves, so we should not be directing them at others.

Of course this is all easier when the children are small. Some people say that as children grow so do the problems and special challenges of the teen years. Having raised three teens and in the process of raising the fourth, I can definitely attest to those challenges. Too many parents make the mistake of waiting till there is trouble in the teen years to address their children's behaviour. All of a sudden the kids are expected to resist peer pressure when they spent their earlier childhood being indulged.

By the time children reach their teen years the pressures have built up mainly from two opposing forces: the expectations of their parents and the expectations of their peers. Peer pressure tends to be anti-establishment. Everything they learned willingly in the elementary years is now rejected as conformist and boring. It is difficult but not impossible for teens to pass through these trials with their religious convictions intact.

As Muslims we have a bit of an advantage in this respect and that comes from fasting in the month of Ramadan. When we fast, we are denying ourselves that which is lawful for the sake of obedience and love of God. Giving up for a short time what is lawful, makes it much easier to give up that which is prohibited. You would think that exposing children to such hardship would make them resentful or rebellious. Not in my experience. In fact, what I've noticed is that those who begin fasting at a young age tend to grow up to be more religious.

When children are small they are often eager to fast because they see it as something the grownups do. They take pride in their accomplishment, knowing full well that it isn't easy to go hungry. It says clearly in the Qur'an and hadith that the purpose of fasting is to learn self-restraint. And in sexual terms young adults who find it hard to abstain are encouraged to fast to keep themselves pure.

As parents, the teen years are the time we need to be most patient and vigilant with them. You have to use tact and diplomacy. Respect them, so they will continue to respect you, but don't be afraid of laying down your authority. Remember that these are the years your child is establishing their identity. These years are some of the hardest they will go through. Their bodies are growing rapidly and emotionally they are grasping towards adulthood. Be ready to talk to them when they are ready to talk. This may occur at inopportune moments. But if you don't drop everything and take time to listen when they want to talk, then the window of opportunity can pass. No child jumps into immorality and depravity. Rather they tend to stray into it. There are warning signs. Look for them and heed them.

Take the time to cool down and think before you react to something they have done, and above all, keep your sense of humour. My parents illustrated this point beautifully when I went through a brief spate of shoplifting. Money was tight when I was growing up and too often my mother would say no when we asked if we could get candy from the candy store. So one day, when no one was looking, I stuck a chocolate bar in my pocket and walked out. The next day I did the same. It got to be a habit but the problem was where to put the candy loot? There was no privacy in my bedroom. My siblings would definitely notice me with candy so I lifted a rock in the flagstone retaining wall and hid my stash in there. One day my younger sister caught me retrieving some candy and asked where I got it from. I lied and told her it was a magic rock and that everyday I just checked underneath it and voila! there was candy. I told her that if she kept this secret I would share candy with her.

Now I had to steal twice as much. But a few days later when we were having a dinner of dillweed and potato curry, my little sister turned up her nose and said, "I wish we could just eat the candy from the magic stone." My mother said, "What magic stone?" I begged my sister, making eyes at her, not to tell, but she blurted out, "The one Rukhsana found. Everyday there's candy underneath it! It's magic." My parents turned very slowly to stare at me. I was expecting to get hit, but my father did no such thing. My parents took me into the room and coaxed me for what felt like hours to tell the truth, to tell them where I got the candy. They weren't going to hit me, but I had to tell the truth. When I did confess, I expected them to break their word and really strike me, but they didn't. They calmly told me I was never to do that again, and why. They reinforced the idea that this was breaking God's laws. I never stole again.

I have often spoken of my own teenage years with my children so they understand that I've been through some of the same things they are struggling with right now. I give them advice when appropriate but do so gently, and don't harp on it, and I always ask for their input concerning changes and arrangements that affect them.

It's important to give your children opportunities to make their own decisions but guide them where necessary. In some of these decisions they will make mistakes, but as long as the mistake isn't life threatening or detrimental to their long-term health let them make the mistake. Making mistakes is integral to learning. What better way for them to make mistakes and learn from them than while still in the relative safety of your home environment? And further to that, when they disappoint you it's best not to suffocate them with reproach. Help them work their way out of it. It is very important to respect a teen's privacy and space, but at the same time listen carefully for inconsistencies in what they say to see if they're trying to deceive you. Encourage them to have their friends over. In fact you should always know who your child's friends are

Ultimately, it is not your job as a parent to live your children's lives for them. They will have to forge their own paths. I always told my children that it wasn't my job to make them Muslim. Only God can give guidance. It is my job to show them the way, and it is their choice whether they will take that way or another path of their choosing.

Islamic Theology and Moral Agency: Beyond the Pre- and Post-Modern

ANVER M EMON

Introduction

The complex relationship between meaning and agency is not something from which we can escape. We confront it each time we are asked to make decisions, whether as individuals or as political communities. For instance, in the so-called Shariʿa Debate in Ontario, Canada, in 2004 and 2005, proponents and opponents of Shariʿa family arbitration were convinced that Shariʿa arbitration was either liberating of or oppressive to the moral agent. But neither actually addressed what Shariʿa was, is, or can be in different times and places. In June 2008, the South Asian Legal Clinic of Ontario organized an international conference where activists and professionals discussed the incidents of forced marriage and strategized methods to combat it. But part of the challenge in combating "forced marriage" is to determine when a marriage is indeed forced, as opposed to arranged or otherwise solemnized. Where cultural norms dictate that parents play a significant role in the matrimonial arrangements of their children, what does it mean to force, let alone to consent to such marriages?

An uncritical acceptance of liberal assumptions of agency covers the underlying frameworks or structures that inform whether and how we make choices. Indeed, I have argued elsewhere that the polemics in the Ontario debate on Shariʿa from both sides failed to account for the specifics of a tradition that structures and frames the way many render their world meaningful.[1] Frameworks of meaning, such as are provided by religion and culture, are embedded in the world we inhabit and are made manifest through the choices we make. They frame the scope (to varying degrees) within which members of those traditions act and render their lives meaningful.

In an essay of this length, I cannot hope to address in any meaningful depth what moral agency means. Rather what I offer is an illustration of how one might appreciate the way different frameworks of meaning may offer alternative and comparative perspectives on moral agency. The central question in this essay is: What does it mean to be a moral agent within the devotional and conceptual framework of Islam?

To attempt an answer to such a question is to immediately subject myself to the critique of selectivity, partiality, and incompleteness. How can I begin to explore such a question given the vast corpus of Islamic intellectual debates over centuries, ranging across the fields of philosophy, theology, law, and ethics? Any attempt to answer definitively such a question, especially within the confines of a short article such as this, is doomed to failure. Yet the question cannot be avoided since the inevitability of living in the world puts us in situations where we must make decisions about how to act. The question of moral agency seems ever present for those interested in the ways in which we render our world meaningful for ourselves. For the purposes of this essay, moral agency is fundamentally tied to our ongoing endeavor to live meaningful lives.[2]

In order to pursue this topic and limit my task in the interest of academic integrity, I offer this essay as a mere illustration of how attention to tradition may illuminate the ways in which the Islamic theological tradition offers competing frames of meaning that influence the way we might understand moral agency. In this article, I explore the language of moral agency in Islamic theology by focusing on a particular premodern debate, namely the debate on free will. On the surface, one stake in the theological debate concerns the power and omnipotence of God. That seems obvious. But from a humanistic perspective, the theological debates implicitly invoke an interest in the meaning and scope of moral agency in the world.

Islamic Theology Debates on Free Will and Determinism

The theological debates on free will and determinism (*qadar*) for some jurists seem intimately connected to the liberty one has to construct moral meaning in life and translate that meaning into norms of behavior using the normative language of Shari'a. For instance, if all things are determined, such as our actions, there is little meaningfulness in exercising rational analysis and investigating the moral significance of different choices in the course of our lives. One could perhaps infer that success and achievement in the world are divine indications or confirmations of salvation in the hereafter. This might offer one route to meaningful moral agency. But arguably such an approach seems to be only a poor end-run around the determinist thesis's implication about our incapacity to create moral meaning and act upon it prospectively. On the determinist view, whether we are good or bad, saved or damned, is a retrospective analysis based on the facts of our past. But the option to choose our path – to make morally meaningful choices – which can affect and alter our future life choices seems outside the framework of the determinist thesis.

The Qur'an contains numerous verses that provide conflicting statements about whether human actions are determined by God or whether individuals exercise free choice. For instance, the Qur'an states: "God leads astray whom He desires and guides whom He desires."[3] In another instance, it states: "Whoever God decides to guide, He opens his heart to Islam. Whoever He decides to lead astray, He makes his heart narrow and constricted."[4] These verses can be read to suggest that whether we are guided or not is the result of divine intervention and not human action. Furthermore, throughout the Qur'an, God is said to have created all that is in existence, suggesting that even an individual's actions are determined by God's will.[5]

On the other hand, the Qur'an also includes verses that suggest individuals have free choice and are rewarded and punished for their choices. For instance, the Qur'an states: "[Every soul] receives [every good] that it earns, and endures [every evil] it earns."[6] The verse implies that we are responsible for our own acts, and are rewarded and punished accordingly. These competing messages in the Qur'an certainly create confusion. The theological debates that arose in the first three centuries of Islamic history illustrate how these verses were used to articulate competing theologies about God's omnipotence and the nature of human action.[7]

For instance, Basran Mu'tazilites held that human beings exercise free will,[8] while the Jabarites endorsed the doctrine of predestination. Both couched the debate in terms of identifying when one has the capacity and power to perform a particular act. These Mu'tazilites argued that our power to act is embedded within us prior to any action we take, and we can freely choose to act without any constraint. The Jabarites argued that prior to our decision to act, we have no power or capacity to decide whether to act or not. Rather, both the power *and* the actual commission of the act arise within us at the same moment, as a matter of God's will. At this point, we cannot choose to act in any contrary way.[9] The Jabarite determinist position emphasized the omnipotence of God: to give human beings free will would implicitly suggest that God does not control or create everything, but rather that we have a competing creative power as well. The Mu'tazilites found the determinist position fundamentally contrary to the justice and goodness of God – both being divine virtues they held in the highest esteem.[10] According to these Mu'tazilites, the injustice of the determinist theory is that we could be judged for our actions despite the fact that we are effectively coerced to perform them. Furthermore, in the event that the act in question is evil, then effectively God is responsible for evil. Neither of these possibilities was acceptable to the Mu'tazilites given their theology of God as both just and good.

The Ash'arite theological school, named after the former Mu'tazilite Abu al-Hasan al-Ash'ari (d. 935–6),[11] attempted to take a middle position, and in doing so introduced the concept of *iktisab*, or acquisition. Under this doctrine, God creates both the act and the power in us to perform the act, although we cannot use that power to pursue a different course of action. By giving us the power to act and thereby take ownership of our action (*iktasaba*),[12] the Ash'arites offered a means by which we could be held morally accountable while still preserving God's justice and omnipotence.

Yet another theological group, the Maturidites, challenged the

Ashʿarites and held that our power to commit an act not only exists before the act, but also includes its opposite. Al-Maturidi (d. 943–947)[13] himself emphasized a human being's choice (*ikhtiyar*) in his affairs, and hence adopted a free will position.[14] But the Maturidites also held that the power to commit an act does not stem from our innate qualities but rather from God, thus preserving God's omnipotence amidst human free choice. We can act as we choose, but we do so in the light of a power created by God. As Abu Hanifa (d. 767) stated, "All acts of people . . . are actually acquired by them and God created all of them by His willfulness, knowledge, decision and power."[15] In other words, humans choose their actions pursuant to a power created by God.[16]

Skeptical of all of these positions, the famous philosopher and jurist Ibn Rushd (Averroes, d. 1198) argued that the Ashʿarite position does not fundamentally depart from the determinist thesis since both views hold that the act and the power to perform the act are determined by God. He ridiculed the concept of *iktisab* as making little difference in the debate between free will and determinism.[17] Instead, he recognized that the different positions were neither right nor wrong; rather that the truth lay in the middle.[18] On the one hand, it would seem trivial to think that God determines every act we choose for ourselves, whether to chew a stick of gum now or later, or buy a cup of coffee on the way to work or in the afternoon. On the other hand, we make these choices within a context that both frames and even limits the scope of our choice. Whether we buy a cup of coffee on the way to work may depend on whether we have been paid recently or have money in our pockets, have a job, or participate in a market economy that offers employment to varying sectors of the labor force. Choices are made within a context or set of circumstances that frame and limit the ambit of choice.

These circumstances are what Ibn Rushd called "external causes" (*asbab kharija*), which structure the range of one's choice. God may give humans the faculty to choose, but God also limits those choices by putting into creation forces or external causes that limit the scope of our choice. "Human actions are neither completely freely chosen, nor purely compelled. They depend on two factors: [1. the exercise] of free will at a particular moment, [2.] as tied to external causes that proceed in a standard fashion."[19] The external causes exist as a matter of divine will, whether as laws of nature, the nature of poverty and wealth, or other such circumstances. In a world in which God is ever present, these structures are a function of God's creative will. Arguably, even when modern theorists remove God from the picture, our commitment to and respect for such structures still remains.[20]

The implications of this brief discussion are significant for those wishing to situate themselves in a framework of meaning that reflects an engagement with the Islamic tradition and their lived reality. Importantly, the imperative to do so is not simply reflected in premodern theological debates, nor even in the Islamic tradition alone. Popular culture reminds us that the imperative to be a moral agent is something we ignore at our peril. For example, the film *The Matrix* presents the protagonist Neo who, throughout the trilogy, grapples with whether his destiny is a function of his free choice, or whether fate or purpose propels him in certain directions that may ultimately force sacrifices he would rather not make. The more we consider ourselves determined by external forces, arguably the more we dilute the creative force of our agency as we engage the world around us. On the other hand, the more we consider ourselves freely acting agents, the more we will consider our meaningfulness in life a product of our own will. Indeed, the structures of everyday life will seem immaterial to our sense of self. Both positions are extreme, and as Ibn Rushd suggested, both seem to miss the point. If we are mindful of Ibn Rushd's position, we must take cognizance of the fact that we are embedded agents. Yet, all three positions are found within the Islamic theological tradition and thus contribute to a fascinating account of a framework that is beset by alternative, competing models, some or all of which may or may not resonate with every person who identifies with the Muslim Islamic faith.

From Theology to Moral Agency

To move from the theological models above to an analysis of the scope of moral agency is not necessarily an obvious one. In the premodern Islamic literary tradition, questions of theology were addressed in the field of *kalam* (dialectic theology), while moral agency might be discussed in various genres ranging from ethics (*akhlaq*) to legal theory. I want to suggest, though, that the move from theology to moral agency is one that we ignore to our own detriment. Premodern Muslim jurists not only recognized the link, but also engaged in fierce debates about the implications of that link on the scope of moral agency.

The fierceness of the debates may also have much to do with the implications on the way we approach disciplines such as Islamic law. To the extent that Islamic law reflects an investigation into the good and the bad, with varying implications on obligation and prohibition, we might consider Islamic legal analysis a subset of the larger category of moral agency.[21] Recall the Shari'a debate in Ontario, Canada. As noted above, proponents and opponents of Shari'a arbitration seemed to share a conception of Islamic law, namely as a code of rules centuries old. Indeed, the content of this code seemed to be so powerfully determinate as to preclude ongoing deliberations about what Shari'a could be in a Canadian liberal polity. In other words, both sides to the debate limited the scope of moral agency in the determination of what Shari'a could be in Canada. Notably, this understanding of Shari'a is not unique to the Canadian context. Currently Muslims in Mindanao (The Philippines), Malaysia, and Indonesia are contending with each other about the content and flexibility of Shari'a. The debates that played out between Muslim groups in Canada are playing out in similar fashion between Muslim groups in other countries. Proponents and opponents of Shari'a both assume Shari'a to be a historical, doctrinally determinate set of rules, with little room for interpretive engagement. Shari'a has become a structure that is so external to the individual and so determinative of legal meaning that it precludes meaningful moral agency by those who identify with the faith and tradition.

To suggest that the free will debate has anything to do with this reductive view of Islamic law may seem hard to follow. Fortunately, Ibn Taymiyya (d. 1328) has illuminated a way for us. According to Ibn Taymiyya, to understand the implications of the free will and determinism debate on moral inquiry, one must recognize that the theological issue occupies two levels. At the first level, the debate is about

God's power. "Qadr is about the power of God ... [God] is the fashioner of all that exists."²² In this sense, Ibn Taymiyya is writing about the *ontology* of God's willfulness, lordship and creative power (*al-mashi'a wa al-rububiyya wa ibtida' al-umur*).²³ However, this ontological power of God does not negate the fact that, at another level, we must understand how God enacts His power upon us.

For Ibn Taymiyya, the second level of the debate concerns the *epistemic* position of individuals trying to understand the divine will and its creative power in terms of the wisdom in creation (*hikma*), the existence of divine commands (*al-awamir al-ilahiyya*), and the purpose of God's commands (*nihayat al-umur*).²⁴ God may be a creative power, but we must understand what that creative power demands of us. As Ibn Taymiyya stated:

> The distinction [between the two levels of *qadar* analysis] leads to [understanding] the difference between benefit and harm, and their causes. This difference is understood by recourse to sensory perception, reason, and scripture, and is agreed upon both by old and recent scholars. It is known by animals and exists in all created things. When we establish the difference between good (*al-muhsanat*) and evil (*al-sayyi'at*) – which is the difference between the good (*hasan*) and the bad (*qabih*) – the difference relates to this [second level of investigation].²⁵

God creates all things; those things may lead to benefit or harm for us. Our knowledge of the good and the bad, the beneficial and the harmful, constitutes indicators of the divine will that we discern for ourselves and thereby act upon, thus taking an active role in rendering our world meaningful for us. By discerning what is beneficial and harmful, we inevitably investigate the good (*hasan*) and bad (*qabih*) to make our conduct in the world morally meaningful.²⁶ The two-level inquiry suggests that, for Ibn Taymiyya, we cannot avoid exerting a degree of moral and interpretive agency; such agency is essential if we are to live meaningful lives within the framework of an all-powerful God.

For Ibn Taymiyya, the most significant things that we must

investigate for understanding the good and the bad are God's express indicators, such as the Qur'an and the Sunna of the Prophet. Indeed, these two sources are foundational to the Islamic faith, and thereby also limit the scope of our moral agency. But not all Muslim jurists limited the scope of moral agency in the same way.

For example, the Hanbali jurist al-Tufi (d. 1316) made considerable room for moral agency in the law, while acknowledging the foundational role of the Qur'an and Sunnah of the Prophet. Of specific interest to him was the following *hadith*: "There is no harm or injury. Whoever causes harm, God will harm him, and whoever causes distress, God will distress him."[27] According to al-Tufi, this *hadith* fundamentally means that no harm befalls someone *as a matter of law* unless a specific indicator requires it.[28] This is not to suggest in absolute terms that the law does not permit harm. Of course, where the law punishes someone, it rightfully imposes pain and harm. But for al-Tufi, the presumptive state of things is that as a matter of law, pain and harm are to be avoided, unless evidence to the contrary exists. Indeed, he held that repudiation of harm and corruption is a general principle of law.[29] This principle defines the purpose of Islamic law and thereby frames the meaning and applicability of any source-text evidence. Consequently, either the requirements from source-texts uphold the good or they do not. If they do not uphold the good (*maslaha*), al-Tufi suggested that they would need to be reinterpreted if we are to ensure the primacy of the good as a default principle in the law.[30] Importantly, by using the notion of *maslaha* to frame the law, al-Tufi empowered us to utilize our moral agency to engage both the source-texts of Islamic law and the context in which we find ourselves to render our legal decisions meaningful.

Conclusion

Although Muslims disagree on the theology of free will or determinism, the purpose of this article has been to illustrate that more is at stake than just debating the omnipotence and the glory of God. Certainly the Islamic conception of God emphasizes His power and authority over all things in creation. But the implications of God's power on the possibility of human moral agency is indeed a corollary issue that raises important questions about the significance of this theological question on the ways we conceptualize our moral agency, and thereby our meaningfulness in the world.

The brief discussion of al-Tufi and Ibn Taymiyya offers two examples of Muslim jurists who recognized the imperative of moral agency. Clearly we all make decisions about the good and the bad all the time. We cannot escape this fact of human existence. Yet for many, those decisions are meaningful to the extent they are framed within a tradition to which they belong, religious or cultural. But if they rely on such traditions to frame their choices, to what extent are they meaningfully acting as agents in the world? If we uncritically adopt a liberal conception of the individual, we may find ourselves vexed by this question. But if we can appreciate how different traditions provide a framework of meaning for moral agents, we may find ourselves in a more suitable position for dialogue across borders that are often perceived rather than real. This brief exploration of both the free will debate in Islamic theology and its link to moral agency has been offered, in part, to foster a dialogue about the ways in which meaning and identity can be framed within the Islamic intellectual tradition. No doubt there are other approaches one could adopt. If anything, perhaps this essay may spark the interest to explore what other approaches might offer.

But this essay has hopefully served another purpose, namely to inspire a more general dialogue across frameworks of meaning – religious, philosophical and otherwise – about what it means to be a moral agent in the world. The possibility of an intellectual connection between premodern Islamic theology and, for instance, contemporary philosophical debates about moral agency can open the door to questions and ideas that cross disciplines, regions, and time periods. Certainly one must avoid the anachronisms that arise from imposing contemporary theoretical frameworks on past traditions that may not have been designed to answer the questions posed by contemporary critical theorists. Nonetheless, this brief exploration of a specific issue in Islamic theology hopefully illustrates the possible fruits of understanding that can arise from exploring how questions of moral agency in one seemingly distinct tradition may nonetheless be framed in ways that resonate with those outside that tradition but who nevertheless are interested in the pursuit of moral meaning in the world today.

Muslim Girl Magazine: Representing Ourselves

AUSMA ZEHANAT KHAN

Introduction

In September 2005, members of our publishing team attended the Islamic Society of North America (ISNA) Convention in Chicago. At that event, they heard many young women speak about their experience of growing up Muslim in North America. A common theme to arise out of these discussions was the pervading sense these young women had that their voices were not included or even recognized in mainstream discourse. The representations they saw of Muslims, and of Muslim women in particular, seemed neither accurate nor realistic. While they couldn't deny the relevance or timeliness of news about political Islam worldwide, they also felt that much of the picture was missing. They were overrepresented in negative and reductive ways but underrepresented or excluded altogether in stories that reflected lived realities.

Where were the stories that were true to their life experiences? Where were the stories that represented how Muslims engaged with their faith and their communities beyond the singular representation of a girl wearing a headscarf? Where were the voices in the middle – of those who did not didactically insist that only the most conservative interpretations and practice of faith were legitimate, or of those who had opted out of faith altogether – a middle group largely ignored both within and outside Muslim communities? In short, the young Muslim women who spoke at ISNA and the girls and young women I had spent most of my life with in different community settings and situations – were correct. The picture of Muslim life in North America was incomplete. The picture of Muslim women, rendered so often in facile stereotypes, was reductive.

The young women we heard from were right to feel neglected, alienated or excluded. A thoughtful, self-critical forum where their voices could be heard and their stories told was urgently needed. *Muslim Girl* magazine came about in response to this need.

I was recruited to take charge of *Muslim Girl* while I was teaching as an Adjunct Law Professor at Northwestern University in Evanston, Illinois. I was teaching courses on international human rights law and the politics of human rights when I was introduced to the publishers by a mutual friend, herself an ardent and outspoken activist on Muslim women's rights. As she described the potential for the magazine to me, ideas I had been considering for the past decade about the necessary evolution of North American Muslim communities began to crystallize. I began to see a very clear connection between the field I had been engaged in for the past eight years, the direction such a magazine might take, and the larger goals it might achieve. My move to the United States in the post-9/11 climate made my sense of urgency to take on this mission to add Muslim voices to mainstream political and cultural discourse all the more compelling. The question was whether it would be possible to do so in a commercial publication aimed at girls and young women while keeping them engaged.

Teaching human rights law, I routinely engage with fiercely intelligent and ethical students who are not interested in easy answers to the complex human rights questions of our times: Darfur, Iraq, Kosovo, Tibet. Given that background, it was not possible to see *Muslim Girl* as merely a publication to make Muslims feel good about themselves or to make non-Muslims feel less afraid of Muslims, both laudable goals yet not nearly ambitious enough. The challenge was to create a publication that could fulfill the needs of its primary audience – a publication that could "enlighten, celebrate and inspire" – while also urging critical introspection, arguing for change where change was needed and confronting assumptions that many Muslims themselves hold about women and girls.

The second, equally compelling challenge was to humanize Muslims to their fellow citizens, especially in a political climate dominated by

Fox News, talk radio, and the rampant fear that a current United States presidential candidate may be Muslim.

This could not be accomplished by a manufactured enthusiasm for all things Muslim or by pointing out the beauties or oft-claimed superiority of the Islamic faith. In my view, these goals could only be accomplished through an editorial mission that was grounded in the reality of how Muslim girls and young women actually lived their lives. The stark truth of these stories would do much to set the record straight and enhance these goals.

Editorial Mission

Raised by deeply observant Muslim parents, I have been a lifelong participant in Muslim community organizations, student groups, mosques, and cultural centres. This participation introduced me to nearly every variant of Islamic thought and practice and gave me a rich appreciation of the diversity of the communities *Muslim Girl* wished to serve and represent. As the editorial team of the magazine began to formulate its mission, it became necessary to put down in writing the principles that would guide our vision. Having witnessed firsthand both community unity and disunity, and having benefited throughout my life from Canada's entrenched commitment to multiculturalism, I sought to bring those lessons into play.

Muslim Girl would encourage real rather than idealized representations of Muslim girls and young women. Any young woman who identified herself as a Muslim would merit inclusion in our publication and as part of our audience. Our publication would promote cultural and religious diversity, mutual tolerance and respect, inclusiveness and dissent. Dress code would be a non-issue for us (in terms of hijab versus non-hijab) and we would represent Muslim girls as they actually were, the focus being on the whole girl: her ideas, ambitions, dreams, hopes, and achievements.

Given that what we most wanted was to open up a space for a multiplicity of Muslim voices to be heard and then to inject those voices into the ongoing national conversation about Muslims and Islam, we developed an editorial mission founded on four key objectives.

First, *Muslim Girl* would tell the stories of Muslim girls and young women in North America. We would express the Muslim girl experience by relating the fears, worries, aspirations, and achievements of Muslim girls who have grown up in North America. Given that the voices of Muslim girls are particularly absent from mainstream media and cultural outlets, we would address that shortfall and present our audience with stories, images, and ideas that accurately and positively represent their values.

Second, our publication would be exceptional in recognizing that young Muslim women are very much part of the North American landscape with a cultural inheritance that is both intrinsically diverse and distinctively North American. Our vision is that Muslim girls are not the inaccessible Other; rather, their commonalities with their non-Muslim peers far outweigh their differences. Acknowledging and celebrating that reality would be a step forward in breaking down barriers between communities and diminishing the impact of negative stereotypes.

A third key objective of *Muslim Girl* magazine would be to educate, inspire and entertain our target audience. We would aim to equip Muslim girls with the tools needed to lead better, more successful lives at every level of their aspirations. Success would be measured not only in terms of outward achievement, but also in terms of improved self-esteem, a richer sense of spirituality, and a deeper engagement with family, community, and society. These themes would also be of appeal to a non-Muslim audience.

Finally, our fourth objective would address a subject not frequently discussed in Muslim homes and community centres – that of the necessity of cultural production. Muslim communities recognize the importance of participation in law, journalism, public policy, and political organizations and there have been significant developments in these areas of community life and in individual career choices. What's less well understood is the role that art and culture play in adding minority voices to the dominant discourse and in helping to shape public attitudes and perceptions.

Art and culture represent the lifeblood of every community and have often served to bring underrepresented and misunderstood voices to the forefront. To that end, a critical part of *Muslim Girl's* editorial content would focus on art, literature, film, television, books, news, and online media. At times this could correspond with a deeper inquiry into the search for beauty and joy in Islam, along with an examination of the reasons for the minimization of artistic aspiration in various Muslim communities.

Our approach to this editorial objective would be three-pronged: (1) we would feature and review the contributions of North American Muslims to the arts and mainstream media (for an example see our profile on Muslim country musician Kareem Salama in the Nov/Dec 2007 issue). (2) We would review depictions of Muslims in popular culture and provide cultural commentary (for example, our assessment of the hit TV series *24*). (3) We would review popular culture and media from the perspectives of Muslim values, since Muslim girls consume and enjoy many of the same cultural products as other North American teens (for examples, see our "Hot List" reviews of the television shows *The Gilmore Girls, Gossip Girl,* and *Smallville* and our arts stories on Harry Potter.)

We set the editorial calendar for the year with these four objectives in mind and measure every story we publish against these criteria.

Stories

I was recently asked to address the California chapter of the National Organization of Women on the subject of "what Muslim women want American feminists to know." In preparation for that talk, I did a quick internet search on the most popular and frequent stories about Muslim women. A sample of the subjects that came up reads as follows:

- the stoning of women for adultery
- female genital mutilation
- the ban on women driving
- honour killings
- forced marriages and early marriage
- the headscarf as a symbol of oppression
- the recent emphasis on the role of Islam in the death of

Mississauga teen Aqsa Parvez
* banning of hijab-wearing soccer players
* the headscarf in fashion
* the niqab (the recent debate on the identity requirement for the Canadian election)

Anecdotal evidence from discussions with Muslim women also brought to light the following assumptions about Muslim women: wearing a headscarf is forced upon girls and women; Muslim girls are timid, shy, and unable to travel, participate in the arts, or engage in athletics; Muslim girls are married off at a disquietingly young age to a partner chosen by their parents and are not free to pursue higher education; Muslim girls are all from immigrant communities and represent a single cultural and historical experience; they have nothing in common with their non-Muslim peers.

Most memorably, a *Syracuse New Times* reporter asked me as a prelude to an interview on *Muslim Girl* magazine: "Muslim girls don't read, do they?" sparking off an animated response from the Syracuse Muslim community.

Against this backdrop, it became vitally important that the kinds of stories we told in *Muslim Girl* reflect a nuanced picture of Muslim girls and women that would defy easy categorization and reflect reality.

Launch Issue

The inaugural issue of *Muslim Girl* was published in January 2007 and we sought to be true to our four key objectives while remaining guided by the principles we articulated at the outset.

On the cover of that issue, and every issue thereafter, we featured a real Muslim girl. Wardah Chaudhary, the cover girl of the first issue is from Oklahoma. She attends an Islamic school and wears a headscarf. She ardently campaigned to be on the cover of our launch issue. Several conversations with this bright, enthusiastic fifteen-year-old convinced us that she was an excellent choice for our first cover. We also decided to make a dramatic statement with that cover by having Wardah hold an American flag and wear red, white, and blue stars on her cheeks. Many people thought she was actually wearing the American flag as her headscarf but we thought the cover made an emphatic enough statement without politicizing her scarf.

What struck me about the discussions at the time was the message that we tried to communicate with the image, which was essentially this: Muslim women are not foreign, Other, or alien, there is an American Islam, and American Muslims are able to reconcile the different, sometimes contradictory aspects of their identities. In many ways, our cheerful, fashion-obsessed cover girl was the perfect exemplar of an "all-American girl."

During the cover shoot, as different members of our team argued for Wardah actually to wear the flag as a headscarf, I was engaged in a discussion with Wardah's father who accompanied her to the photo shoot as her chaperone. I had already made the decision that putting the flag on Wardah's head would be needlessly inflammatory as it conflated two highly charged political symbols (the American flag and the Muslim veil), but it was enlightening to debate with Mr Chaudhary about the negative repercussions the image might generate within Muslim communities – not because of the American flag per se but because of the American flag worn *as a headscarf*. For example, we were both concerned that an American flag on the head of a Muslim girl might be read as a symbol of colonization: i.e. American power imposed on the Muslim world, an image especially troubling in the context of the invasion of Iraq. A symbol of colonization imposed on a girl might be doubly offensive, given that Muslim communities are particularly sensitive about depictions and representations of women. The subtext could easily be that the "West" is saying it has conquered "our women." It seemed likely that read this way, the image would trigger a disproportionately negative or outraged reaction.

Interestingly, Mr Chaudhary had no objection to the flag itself and believed that American citizens were and should be proud citizens of the United States. He thought the stars on Wardah's cheek and the flag in her hand were a strong means of conveying a sense of American Islam and of Muslim belonging in America. The flag worn as hijab was a step too far in his view, because it was a direct association with the United States government and its policies in Iraq, Afghanistan, and elsewhere in the Muslim world.

My secondary concern had more to do with faith than politics. The girls and women who choose to wear a headscarf often view this choice as a symbol of their complete and utter submission to God. Using the flag as the headscarf would turn that choice into a political debate and remove it from the personal and spiritual realm (notwithstanding the reality that some Muslim women and girls do wear the headscarf as a political statement.) I could foresee an interpretation of this image as attempting to render a political or nationalist ideal superior to faith or God. This was not the statement we were trying to make and would have been antithetical to our goal of showcasing a lived reality of Islam very much grounded in American culture and the American milieu.

In the end, the cover image and story "Growing Up American" were more than enough to provoke the kind of discussion and press coverage we had hoped to generate – stories not about the veil or the politicization of the veil, but about the girls themselves and their place in America.

Similarly in that issue, our attempts to show a more nuanced picture of Muslim life included stories on a Canadian Muslim hockey player, an award-winning all-girls basketball team from Atlanta, Georgia, an Indiana Muslim girl who had served two years in the Peace Corps in Malawi, and a "Woman to Watch" profile on BBC News anchor Mishal Husain.

The interior visuals featured girls who wear headscarves and girls who don't. The policy for subsequent covers similarly has been to alternate between choosing girls who wear headscarves and those who don't and to try and represent girls from as many different ethnic backgrounds as possible. On our memorable Sept/Oct 2007 Ramadan cover, we featured two girls side by side – one veiled and one without a veil.

These images served as notice of our intent to remain inclusive and to respect different approaches to the practice of faith. Initially, the lack of uniform hijab among the girls represented in the magazine generated a storm of letters – both from young girls and older readers, male and female – insisting that the only possible representation of Muslim girls and women should be of girls "properly covered" in headscarves. These letters were frequently published and answered in the "Muslim Girl Mailbox" and in one issue, a "Qur'an Notes" column was devoted to the question of hijab. And then we set it aside, as a distracting issue of minor importance and continued with our stated objectives.

Of great insight and encouragement to us were the many letters and comments we received from young Muslim women all across the faith spectrum, celebrating and supporting our position – insisting they had no difficulty accepting that their sisters might view this issue differently than they did and nonetheless deserved their respect. And many young women took the position that we did – that dress code was a nonissue, a private matter and that Muslims had far more pressing matters to turn their attention to.

We endeavoured to keep our attention on those pressing matters. In terms of arts and culture, our launch issue included a major feature on the hit show *24* that both analyzed its artistic merit as a well-produced, well-written, and superbly acted show and that took it to account for its continued depiction of Arabs and Muslims as terrorists. Ultimately, our review highlighted the dangers of such representation in inflaming public feeling against Muslims, while also acknowledging the steps the show had taken to mitigate that possibility.

Subsequent Issues

Subsequent issues of *Muslim Girl* have highlighted Muslim writers like Randa Abdel-Fatteh, Rajaa Alsanea, Ibtisam Barakat, Mohja Kahf, Yasmine and Dilara Hafiz, and Rima Khoreibi, and the funny, illuminating and deeply humanizing stories they tell. Lupe Fiasco, Brother Ali, Outlandish, Taleb Kweli, Ani Zonneveld, Native Deen, Sami Yusuf, Sara Siddiqui, Usra Leedham, Neenah, spoken word artist Sofia Baig, *Little Mosque on the Prairie* and *Aliens in America* have all been reviewed or featured in our pages. We've drawn attention to aspects of popular culture of special interest to our readers, such as the films *Persepolis, Blackboards, At Five in the Afternoon,* and *American Ramadan* and online media such as sunnisisters.com, altmuslim.com, maniacmuslim.com, islamicanews.com, ninjabi.com, junnah.com, muslimhiphop.com, and mynaraps.com.

By keeping Muslim voices in the arts front and centre, our hope is to introduce them to a larger audience, to educate Muslim girls about pursuing a career in the arts and to showcase a side of Muslim life that is rarely seen in mainstream media, despite breakthrough television shows like *Little Mosque on the Prairie* and *Aliens in America*. We asked ourselves the question: could you look at your Muslim neighbour in the same light after you had taken in the comedy routine of Azhar Usman in "Allah Made Me Funny"? Our answer was that for immediate impact and bridge-building, nothing can surpass the arts.

In terms of critical introspection, we launched *Muslim Girl* with a regular department called "GirlSpace" that asked Muslim girls across North America to write in and comment on how female-friendly their local mosques were. We knew alienation from the mosque was a central complaint for many young girls – whether it was the dark, exclusionary entrances, the reduced, uncomfortable prayer space, or the sometimes regressive and disenfranchising nature of Friday sermons. By giving girls a place to voice constructive criticism and approbation of mosques that did include women as part of the community, we hoped to perform a vital public service along with re-engaging interest in the mosque as a centre of community life. Initially, many young women wrote along these lines but in subsequent issues young women also wrote positively about their experiences during Ramadan and any occasion of crisis in their local communities.

Other features addressed issues that require more open discussions between Muslim girls and their parents, including independent career choices, going away to school, dating and relationships with the opposite sex, conversion, peer pressure, the prom, marriage, and the right to make choices about how to practice one's faith.

Human rights features included stories on Afghanistan (the theme of the March/April 2007 issue), Bosnia (the anniversary of the Srebrenica massacre in the July/August 2007 issue), child victims of the war in Iraq (the Sept/Oct 2007 Ramadan issue), inter-faith work in Indonesia, the wars in Lebanon and Darfur, and the human rights crisis in Palestine (all in the Nov/Dec 2007 "Girls Go Global" issue). Uniquely, these stories were all told from the perspectives of Muslim girls who had a point of entry or engagement into the issues, primarily, although not exclusively, through their perspectives as Americans.

Sports features included soccer, volleyball, basketball, and hockey players, alongside karate, aikido, and figure-skating champions. Muslim girls also wrote of their travel experiences, often coupled with human rights work, to countries such as Egypt, Brazil, Turkey, Morocco, Malawi, Saudi Arabia, and Yemen.

Our role-model feature "Women to Watch" has focused on accomplished Muslim women and included such distinguished luminaries as BBC anchor Mishal Husain, Afghan presidential candidate Dr Massouda Jalal, *Little Mosque* creator Zarqa Nawaz, Malaysian human rights activist Zainah Anwar, ISNA President Dr Ingrid Mattson, Moroccan Olympic champion and Minister of Sport Nawal El Moutawakel, and Afghan-Canadian journalist Hamida Ghafour who routinely travels to war zones.

In sum, *Muslim Girl* presents a picture of Muslim life and lived values that bears little relation to the popular news stories of the day without neglecting the real problems and challenges facing Muslim communities. While doing our best to lead on issues we consider critical (Darfur, Afghanistan, female empowerment and independence), we also aim to remain true to the core values of our readers who have made the decision to identify themselves as Muslim.

We recognize that there is a rich heritage of diversity in the practice of Islam and we see that in the lives and stories of our readers and of the girls and young women we feature in our pages. The reality is that there are so many interesting and eye-opening stories about Muslim girls and young women that we can't cover them all. We recognize the necessity of representing these voices and adding them to the ongoing national conversation about Muslims, in the hopes of moving that conversation forward in a positive and enriching direction.

Conclusion

My role as the Editor in Chief of *Muslim Girl* has been an immensely fulfilling one. I have learned much from the creativity, resilience, and resourcefulness of young women from Muslim communities across North America. Wherever *Muslim Girl* has been invited to participate in and represent local community groups, we have benefited from hearing the stories of young women who are deeply engaged with their families and communities, who strive to better themselves in all aspects of their lives, and who sincerely desire to make a contribution to the world around them. These are the stories I believe are worth telling and celebrating, without denying that there remains a great deal of work to be done within our communities and at *Muslim Girl*.

We have to challenge ourselves to speak incisively and honestly about the exclusion of women and girls from participation in community life, particularly that centered around the mosque, with an understanding of the egalitarian and justice-based principles of our faith and the continued need for tolerance and respect of others whose ideas and practices differ from our own.

Being self-critical without contributing to inflammatory and ill-judged attitudes about Islam and Muslims is always a difficult line to walk but it's a necessary task if we are to preserve our editorial integrity and if our communities are to move forward. From the many stories we have covered about remarkable young Muslim women in North America, I am confident that this is a challenge we can continue to navigate with success.

Towards a Dialogical Discourse for Canadian Muslims

AMIN MALAK

> What this country did to us, it did to itself.
> JOY KOGAWA, *Obasan*

Let me begin with a heart-warming incident that should inspire any caring Canadian. In the turbulent days immediately following the 9/11 horror, the leaders of the Jewish and Christian communities of Edmonton realized that the Muslims of Alberta's capital were in for a rough time. In an impressive gesture of solidarity, the leaders of the two Abrahamic faiths, accompanied by senator Doug Roche and religious studies professor Earle Waugh, went to Al-Rasheed mosque, the largest in the city, and publicly attended the Friday prayer. Some joined the worshippers in the prayer hall – normally accessible only to Muslims. A minister from the United Church of Canada, Bruce Miller, even prayed with the Muslim worshippers, emulating their ritualistic gestures: bowing, kneeling, standing, and mouthing the Muslim article of faith.

Only a confident, caring culture can perform such an elegant proactive gesture. Only a genuinely generous community appreciates the generosity of other communities extending such a warm hand.

That Islam and Muslims are now part of Canada's constituent mosaic is an indisputable reality. Given the diversity of perspectives and voices emanating from Muslims living in the country, a language of understanding and respect must emerge, evolve, and flourish to embrace the precious reality of the Muslim strand interwoven into the Canadian fabric. Many well-intentioned Canadians, Muslims and non-Muslims, worked hard to turn this transformative presence into a meaningful reality, irrespective of occasional clouds of misunderstanding and tension.

Despite its acknowledged imperfections, Canada remains the best space and environment for Muslim culture and identity to flourish in a pluralist, secular state. This means that the Muslim communities should be able to participate in Canadian life in a way that does not violate the ethos of the cultural mosaic that characterizes Canada and does not violate the pivotal values of Islam. This applies to other groups and their faiths too. What joins the Muslims to their Canadian co-citizens, in all their diversities, is far greater than what divides them. This is a critical fact that all concerned need to underscore.

While Canadian Muslims, like all the other constituent components of Canadian society, are not monolithic and can never be reduced to one voice, attitude, or organization, they nevertheless may be collectively in need of a grounded, enlightened approach to comprehend and respond engagingly to their reality in the country. As I see it, such an approach has to be dialogical, interactive, and transactional. Canadian Muslims are now an integral, integrating part of the Canadian reality and as such they both contribute and receive. The reciprocal exchanges – material, social, and cultural – are enriching, meaningful, and rewarding for all involved. Such an organic dynamic has to be rooted in mutual respect, governed by shared responsibilities, and directed towards an inclusive, wholesome vision of harmony and solidarity.

Condemnation of Terrorism

Given the charged global geopolitical condition today, especially when outrageous crimes are committed in different parts of the world by some fringe fanatical groups in the name of Islam, it is crucial for the Canadian polity and media to dissociate Canadian Muslims from the heinous phenomenon of terrorism. As Canadians, we embrace a culture of equity, justice, and respect for the law, and accordingly reject guilt by association. Just because some terrorist groups elsewhere in the world cloak themselves in the banner of Islam does not mean that they represent *all* Muslims. On the other hand, it is equally crucial that Muslims in Canada continue to take an unequivocal stance against terrorism committed elsewhere in the name of their religion. Not only do Canadian Muslims have to distance themselves from horrendous crimes against innocent lives, they also should condemn them in the strongest terms. It is indeed regrettable that terms like "Islamic terrorism" and "Muslim terrorists" have become common currencies in the global media. Those using these terms unadvisedly are unaware of the poignant oxymoron involved in them. Islam, whose linguistic etymology denotes "peace," values human life, irrespective of faith (or lack of it), gender, race, or ethnicity. Murdering innocent human beings, as is done by the so-called suicide bombers, is indisputably un-Islamic. In Islam, no one can arrogate to him/herself the province to speak in the name of Allah and issue edicts demonizing others and sanctioning the spilling of their blood. Exploding civilian planes in midair, indiscriminately bombing buildings where innocent people gain their livelihood, beheading hapless hostages, and mutilating human beings are all acts completely incompatible with Islam's cherished and manifest principles. Within such a confirmed context, one needs to recognize the undeniable fact that the absolute majority of Canadian Muslims are hard-working, law-abiding citizens of the country. Thus, they should never be associated with terrorism or even be suspected of being in sympathy with it.

Such a misplaced identification evokes the injustices meted out to Canadian citizens of Japanese origin after Japan's attack on Pearl Harbour in 1941. Then, the Canadian government's misguided policy suspected its own citizens of being in sympathy with Japan's expansionist aggressions during the Second World War. (The hurt and suffering of the Japanese Canadians during this dark period of our history is captured movingly in Joy Kogawa's novel, *Obasan*.) To its credit, Canada had the courage to offer a collective national apology for so appallingly questioning the loyalty of its own citizens. Moreover, any misplaced association of Canadian Muslims with terrorists would render a great service to the so-called Jihadists who strive to tie Islam to violence and would exploit any form of discrimination or persecution, real or perceived, as an opportunity for recruiting disenchanted, disgruntled persons.

Isolationism Versus Engagement

While some Muslims were living in Canada in the years preceding its official founding in 1867, they began arriving in large numbers only in the last five decades, thanks principally to Pierre Trudeau's visionary multicultural policies. As such, Canadian Muslims cannot afford to isolate themselves from their fellow citizens. Being here for all immigrants means engagement with new realities, transacting with different people, and facing paradigms of conduct quite different from their cultures of origin. For a meaningful immersion in the new reality, newcomers and their recipient communities have to undergo processes of adjustment, which might involve moments of tension and misunderstanding. However, over time and after the enlargement of the circles of interaction, a *modus vivendi* emerges, whereby patterns of mutual cooperation develop. Any ethnic or cultural community that rejects cooperation with the larger society runs the risk of living on the margin. This point becomes especially pertinent to some individuals who come under the spell of the isolationist ideology encouraged by extremist Muslim groups.

The simplistic clichés of the so-called Muslim fundamentalism, rooted mainly in retrograde, puritanical Wahhabism of the Arabian Peninsula and propagated by petrodollars, advance a violent politicized version of Islam. Essentially, Muslim fundamentalism is an anti-intellectual trend that reifies the faith and engenders social and cultural paralysis. Islam, both as faith and culture, is too dynamic, compassionate, and sophisticated to be truncated and debased to a few reductionist slogans. The stance of Muslim fundamentalists – anti-Western and even anti-all-other Muslims who do not subscribe to their rigid, one-dimensional appropriation of the faith – damages the objective reality of Canadian Muslims engaged in quotidian transactions with people shaped by other traditions. It does not recognize or allow for open and fresh patterns of engagement different from its loud, intolerant mode of demagoguery. If the presence of Muslims in Canada has been the success that it is perceived to be, it is mainly due to their normal transactional engagements with other components of

the Canadian mosaic. Muslims have been contributing to building a Canadian civilization based on cooperation amongst all the country's constituent communities. This creative convergence of energies is inspired by shared values of acceptance and respect for the diversity of all our cultural and religious source traditions. As a sharp contrast to the fundamentalist rejectionist stance, let us recall the Sufi poet Jalaluddin Rumi's inclusive, embracing call to all:
Come, come, whoever you are.
Wanderer, idolator, worshipper of fire,
Come even though you have broken your vows a thousand times,
Come, and come yet again.
Ours is not a caravan of despair.

The Role of the Intellectuals

Being a heterogeneous community, Muslims in Canada manifest a range of cultural and educational backgrounds. A certain segment of them are highly educated, forming a discernible professional class. The Muslim educated class can play a mediating role between a community deeply nostalgic about its cultural and spiritual inspirations, rooted in the Middle East, Africa, or South Asia, and their Canadian milieux, shaped and coded by a modern secular state. Here we need to recall Antonio Gramsci's concept of the "organic intellectual," who essentially integrates his or her personal fate with that of the dispossessed and marginalized, thus assuming a critical social function. Informed and grounded, the concerned mediating intellectual can be the progressive voice asserting the enlightened, compassionate values of Islam. As well, such an intellectual has to take public and private stands according to the dictates of his or her conscience and convictions. The intellectual needs to be aware and make members of the Muslim communities aware of Canada's founding values that guarantee freedoms of both faith and expression. At times such a mediating operation becomes hard and frustrating, but it has to be undertaken.

Curiously, however, in the last few decades there emerged a regrettable phenomenon whereby a few Muslims undertook to attack Islam in their writing in sensational and provocative ways, becoming North American celebrities overnight. Regrettably, such anti-Islam writers are guaranteed immediate publicity in the prominent fora of Western media, based not on the merit, veracity, or depth of their claims, but on the saleable sensationalism that panders to popular prejudice. As many Muslim intellectuals already know, the surest way for a Muslim writer or academic to get noticed by Western media and publishing houses is to publicly attack Islam, from within so to speak. In a sense, they are encouraged to become what the late Edward Said has labelled, in reference to VS Naipaul's denigrating writings about third-world cultures, "witness[es] for the Western prosecution" (53). This inordinate and undeserved publicity given to such media-savvy, comprador intellectuals, serving as native informers, in turn creates cynicism among Muslims and exacerbates isolationist tendencies. As a valid principle, communities should have the courage and confidence to tolerate criticism from within so long as it is done in the spirit of enlightenment and service towards the public good. Discerning distinction should be made between serious, thoughtful critique and sensational, publicity-hungry superficialities pandering to the prejudices of Western dominant discourses. It is odd to see the Canadian media falling into this practice, so common in the US, especially in neoconservative circles and think-tanks, who embrace and financially support any Muslim from anywhere in the world who lashes out at Islam and Muslim cultures, justifiably or not.

If Canadian institutions care to preserve their integrity and inculcate the spirit of empathy and understanding, then they should pause and ponder the legitimacy and benefit of such a practice. The danger is that a few media-savvy individuals can easily exploit this tendency of embracing anti-Islam, "Muslim" writers and promptly putting them on lucrative speaking circles simply because they are controversial enough for a trusting, uninformed audience. Generating controversy, grabbing headlines, and producing racy sound bites should never be seen as marks of depth or excellence, even when done within the purview of freedom of opinion.

This raises the issue of who speaks for whom. Muslims need to speak for themselves in their diversity and heterogeneity. They need savvy, sensitive voices that simultaneously reflect the civilizational face of Islam and comprehend the Canadian traditions of civil exchange, nonviolence, and multiculturalism.

Islam in Canadian Media

In a country inhabited and developed mostly by immigrants, whether recently or centuries ago, it is healthy for everyone to know something about the heritage, ethos, and sensitivities of others. This awareness broadens our minds, subtly expanding and cross-fertilizing our perceptions of each other and who we are. As Thomas Dewar once put so beautifully, "Minds are like parachutes: they only function when they are open."

Despite Muslims' roots dating back to more than a century in Canada, despite their number in Canada approaching a million, and, more importantly, despite Islam being constantly in news headlines, it is surprising that not much gets told here about the genesis and spread of the world's second largest religion. Apart from exotic and sensational stories, there is a dearth of profound and serious knowledge about Islam that is available in the Canadian media, educational institutions, and official policy pronouncements. Canadian Muslims may be partly responsible for such a gap in the Canadian collective consciousness. However, as a commitment to the common good, it is incumbent on Canadian media establishments, educational institutions, and multicultural organizations to desensationalize and de-exoticize this faith, and to explain it lucidly and in depth. This would open up the space to reflect the diversity of perspectives within the cultures and civilizations of Islam, while foregrounding its common roots with its two sister Abrahamic faiths (Judaism and Christianity) and its many shared values concerning virtue, compassion, generosity, and so forth, with Indigenous spirituality, Hinduism, Buddhism, and other faiths. What combines and connects these different faiths far outweighs what divides them. In this respect, I recall the principle articulated by Imam Ali, the Prophet's cousin and the fourth Righteous Khaleefa, in his letter to his *Wali* (proconsul) in Egypt instructing him how to treat his subjects: "Remember that people are of two kinds: either a brother in faith or an equal in creation" (my translation). The import of this inspiring statement is that all people, irrespective of varied differentiating markers, share something cardinal: their humanity.

The Culture of Pluralism

As a mosaic of cultures and a community of communities, Canada stands out as a shining example to other nations and states. Being proverbially modest and self-effacing, we as Canadians are fully aware of our feet of clay: we candidly recognize and reflect upon our historical errors and present problems: for example, the treatment of our Aboriginal people, the internment of our citizens of Japanese origin during the Second World War, and the intermittent tensions between the Québécois and the rest of Canada. Nonetheless, as a functioning democratic nation we are doing quite well, compared to many parts of the world. Some of the problem areas, subject to periodic carnage, fall in Muslim lands: Kurdistan, Afghanistan, Bangladesh, Chechnya, Darfur, and Palestine. This undeniable fact provided Samuel Huntington with the dubious alibi to claim that "Islam has bloody borders" (35).

Canada's multiculturalism, despite its imperfections, has been instrumental in preserving the heritages of many individuals and communities. Mutual respect and openness have allowed many to be proud of who they are as Canadians, while maintaining the cultural roots that connect them with their ethnic and national communities elsewhere in the world. Ideally, there should be no contradiction and conflict of loyalties. Our multiculturalism is a sign of openness, strength of conviction, and surety of national identity as a country. We are a model of a democracy functioning harmoniously and evolving continuously to adapt to new realities and challenges. What keeps this process healthy and robust is the principle of equality amongst all the constituent components of the Canadian family and the spirit of respect for each other. Given our current conflict-ridden world, Canadian harmony and equilibrium might be tested at times but we strive, despite odds, to keep it nonviolent, at times even civil, within the Canadian family.

One of the sterling benefits of our acceptance of and respect for each other is that our national identity becomes continually enlarged and our perspectives and heritages become intermixed. For Canadian Muslims, as indeed for all Canadians, such cross-fertilization is not a diminishment of loyalties to their cultural heritages but an enrichment of new and evolving identities that are bound to contain within them gestures, symbols, and attitudes coming from other Canadians.

The Status of Muslim Women

Women in Canada, at least in theory, are accorded equality in education, employment, and opportunity to flourish. Canadian feminists might point out many grievances and sexist practices, overt or subtle, that still persist. However, compared to the conditions of women in many Muslim societies, Canadian Muslim women certainly have better chances than their Muslim sisters in those societies, where patriarchy and oppression are regrettably still the norm and where the chances for women to assert themselves and enjoy rights and opportunities equal to men are severely circumscribed. One need only to recall the horror of life for Muslim women under the Taliban tyranny in Afghanistan or under any theocratic or semi-theocratic regimes like the Sheikhdoms of the Arab-Iranian Gulf. Even under nontheocratic regimes, the condition of women is never rosy. Instances of forced marriages, wife battering, child abuse, and, worse, so-called honour killing are not unusual. As well, girls are often denied equal access to education and women workers and professionals are not treated with equity and esteem.

I am quite aware that other Muslim scholars and feminist intellectuals interpret violence as it occurs within Muslim communities differently (Razack, 131). My position in this specific situation stems from a candid, self-critical approach that skirts the culturalist traps of polarizing binary oppositions, stigmatizing Muslims, or denigrating Islam. Moreover, I believe that any dialogical discourse about the condition of Canadian Muslims should be confident and sophisticated enough to espouse continual refinement and rethinking in light of altered realities in an ever-evolving world. In a sense, such an approach is rooted in the Muslim practice of *ijtihad* (interpretative rethinking in light of new phenomena), which affirms the flexibility of Islam's humane, civilizational ethos.

Muslim women, whether in Canada or elsewhere, should never be patronized: they need solidarity, not condescension; encouragement, not pity. They need not be stereotyped into descriptions not their own. They are neither doormats, nor weaklings: they pursue their just struggle according to their own visions and within the contexts of their own culture and conditions. As I have argued in my book about Muslim narratives, Muslim women writers recognize that Islam is an active, relevant agent to be involved with and worked through: "for them, the discourse of liberation passes not through ridiculing or rejecting their Islamic heritage, but through appealing to its most enlightened and progressive tradition" (149). Within such a perspective, Muslim women activists aim at reclaiming their heritage by, among other things, highlighting the leadership role of many pioneering Muslim women, starting with Khadeedja, the Prophet's first wife, whose support was critical in Islam's nascent days. They strive, as well, to give a gendered, woman-friendly interpretation of the holy texts and traditions. In their inclusive praxis, they solicit the support of progressive male Muslims to combat the cruelty and excesses of patriarchy and its arrogant, oppressive, and self-serving discourses.

The anomaly here is that many Canadian Muslim men may continue to adhere to attitudes and practices that were acceptable in their countries of origin and try to transplant them into Canada. What was possibly suitable there may not be appropriate here and now. As well, some Muslim men might feel threatened by women's empowerment accorded by Canadian laws, institutions, and social norms. Denigrating and abusing women is simply intolerable here and, significantly, counter to the Islamic concepts of '*Adle* (justice) and equity. The invocation of a medievalist cultural heritage cannot be accepted as an alibi to curtail women's rights. Cultural norms and practices are never static and cannot be anchored in tradition exclusively. Change is a *sine qua non* for any vibrant civilization and those who resist change are in denial of the spirit of the age in which they live. The innovations of science, the acceleration of technology, and the advances of social sciences all create a constant flux in normative values. They necessitate continual adjustments of human mindsets and individual behaviour. The anachronistic, socio-cultural attitudes, customs, and practices, insofar as they contradict basic Canadian values or violate Canadian laws, have to be abandoned or changed to accord with the current dispensations of the land.

Final Thoughts

As a secular country, Canada provides the best environment for its citizens to enjoy their religious freedom. Our *Charter of Rights and Freedoms*, as well as our democratic institutions and multicultural tradition, guarantee that. Canadian Muslims have an opportunity to flourish culturally, spiritually, and materially. On the other hand, Canada is indeed enriched by the injection of Muslim ethos, values, and traditions. Canada is not Islam's Other, nor is Islam Canada's Other. Islam is now part and parcel of the Canadian fabric. Yes, there have been moments of tension and dispute, such as during the controversies surrounding Salman Rushdie's *Satanic Verses*, the offensive Danish cartoons, the 9/11 backlash, and the Shari'ah law debates in Ontario. But these crises never developed into widespread violence or state-sanctioned transgressions. This in itself is a testament to our national maturity and cohesion. Will there be other problems down the road? For sure, but that would be nothing but a family affair. So long as we do not lose sight of our dialogical, reciprocal responsibilities towards each other, rooted in respect and empathy, the complex and challenging ideals of diversity, harmony, and cohesion are ever achievable and noble.

Islamic Authority: Changing Expectations Among Canadian Muslims

KARIM H KARIM

This essay discusses some of the ways in which Canadian Muslims are rethinking the concept of Islamic authority. It draws from the author's research project, which also deals with similar developments in the USA and the UK.[1] The evidence from the project's focus group discussions and interviews held with Muslims in the three countries has shown that respondents expected their leaders to have knowledge of Western societies, to be engaged in a practical way with their communities, and to adopt critical approaches to the understanding of Islamic tradition.[2]

Contemporary conditions have substantially altered the assumptions under which traditional Islamic authorities have operated for several generations. It is not only the circumstances produced by modernity and migration, but also the educational and technological advances enjoyed by Muslims, as well as the conditions produced by globalization, which have transformed the expectations that adherents have of their leaders. The faithful no longer continue to think of traditional authorities in the same manner as in the past. This appears to be happening because they tend to have more education than religious authorities, enjoy access to primary intellectual sources of Islamic traditions, continually come into contact with new ideas, and are able to use communication technologies to discuss religious issues over vast distances. This essay seeks to examine the ways in which Muslims in Canada are changing the implicit criteria by which they assess the validity of Islamic authority.

According to Khaled Abou El Fadl, a University of California professor, the idea of an "Islamic authority" is often transformed into a "juristic concept of authority [that] has become a firmly embedded part of Islamic dogma" (2001, 31). Dominant Muslim discourses[3] adhere to the permissible and impermissible in Islamic law. It is those with traditional religious training who have had the authority to adjudicate on these issues. For centuries, these *ulama* (religious scholars) have had the institutional legitimacy to interpret scripture in order to make rulings on issues from contemporary life that are brought before them.[4] According to Mohammed Arkoun, professor emeritus at the Sorbonne University in Paris, the early period of Muslim history "sustained a rich theoretical and practical debate in the dialectic, pluralist, dynamic context" which, after the fourteenth century CE (eighth century AH), was replaced by "poor, dogmatic, local discussions and views" on varied matters of Islamic conduct and thought (2002, 208). Whereas this may be a broad generalization, the general tendency among a significant proportion of Muslims has been to refrain from critically challenging either the received wisdom of ages past or to question the authority of established religious leadership. Even though the gates of *ijtihad* (reasoning) were not completely closed, the predominant stance was that of *taqlid* (conformity). The primary source of opposition to established religious leadership, in the form of Islamism,[5] promotes even greater conformism. However, this essay demonstrates that critical debate regarding the nature of religious authority is taking place in Muslim communities in Canada.

Muslims in Western countries not only face the challenges of dealing with a social setting in which their religion is relatively new, they also tend to lack strong institutional structures to which they can turn for support.[6] Additionally, the fast pace of technological and social change continually raises ethical problems that have not appeared previously in human history. Those who have come from countries with well-established religious institutions recall the ways in which issues of faith were addressed. A problem would usually be discussed with the local imam who would issue a legal opinion (*fatwa*) on the matter. Whereas a number of Muslims living in the West continue this practice, many others have become dissatisfied with it. They question the familiarity of imams, who are often "imported" from Muslim homelands, with Western contexts of life. Some even criticize their lack of intellectual capacity to engage with contemporary issues. Muslim scholars with academic training in Islamic studies, especially those who have studied in both Western and traditional institutions, appear to be regarded as more authoritative than traditional imams by an increasing number of the Muslim faithful living in the West. Their familiarity with Western social conditions, institutions, philosophy, and history are viewed as essential to providing reliable advice. The ability to communicate effectively, in person and through various media, is another key criterion for competent religious leadership.

Dale F Eickleman and Jon W Anderson refer to "an emerging Muslim public sphere" in "Muslim majority states and Muslim communities elsewhere" (2003, 1). They comment on how "mass education, new messages, and new communication media" (ibid 16) have vastly increased the numbers of Muslims who are aware of and engaged in discussions of issues that were previously viewed as belonging to intellectual elites. Eickleman and Anderson see these developments as contributing to a growth of Muslim civil societies. Some Muslims in the West have sought to deal actively with the larger society through a contemporary engagement with Islamic sources.

The empirical evidence presented here is based on the findings of focus group discussions conducted with Muslims in Ottawa in March 2004 and Montreal in July 2004. Each session had 13 participants, with representation from both genders, ages ranging from 18 to 70, and ethnic origins from the Middle East, South Asia, Europe, Africa, and South-East Asia, and diverse socio-economic classes. The participants were students, working professionals, and retirees in fields such as engineering, medicine, architecture, media, public administration, and education. The participants came from the Sunni and Shia branches of Islam. Their views are discussed below; however, the individuals are identified only by their initials in order to maintain their privacy.

The Importance of Cultural Context

At the beginning of both sessions, each focus group participant was asked to name who had influenced his or her thinking about Islam. The interlocutors named Muslim and non-Muslim academics specializing in Islamic studies and other areas, religious leaders, artists, institutions, parents, political leaders, historical figures, the Prophet Muhammad, as well as Allah. Among the reasons given for being drawn to specific persons were the institutions in which they were trained, their ability to reach out effectively to Muslim audiences, their accessibility to their constituents, experience in Western environments, open-mindedness, a balanced outlook, practicality, activism, commitment to Islam, and appropriate uses of the media. Several participants cited intellectuals who they thought most closely reflected their own sectarian and cultural identities, but some of these very persons also referred to others outside their groups, including non-Muslims. A number of respondents indicated how they themselves turned to different figures with the passing of time, and others discussed how the intellectuals themselves had changed.

The widest consensus was on the need for religious leaders to have familiarity with the local conditions of Western societies; they were consistently criticized for not having sufficient knowledge of the local language (English or French) and having rigid traditionalist attitudes.[7] A number of discussants in the various focus groups also cited these imams' lack of familiarity with the cultural norms in the place to which they had been assigned. They were described as being out of touch with the needs of their flock. MK remarked near the end of the Montreal session:

> [M]y ultimate fantasy would be to find an imam who gives a *khutbah* in a Friday mosque who happens to be someone who goes out to work from nine to five, takes the bus, is dealing with his kid who is picking up a marijuana joint at the age of thirteen. This is the kind of person that I want instructing me on Friday, not speaking to me about the battles that we won 1200 years ago.

The reality, according to DO, who participated in the Ottawa discussion, was far from such an ideal. She said that

> Most of them [Muslims] are listening to ... what their local imam is saying. And, most of these local imams don't have an

education. For example, some of them, they haven't even had a type of education when it comes to *Shariah*. Yet, they're issuing *fatwas* and they're issuing, you know, judgments here and there.... right now ... I find the local imams have much more power than any scholars.

This interlocutor makes an interesting distinction between the local imams, who are not considered to be learned, and "scholars."

There has been a widespread recognition of the problem of the cultural illiteracy of "imported imams" and some Muslim institutions in the United Kingdom and the United States are making efforts towards addressing this problem. The Muslim College in London seeks to train imams in a contemporary Western context and the Islamic Foundation located near Leicester offers a diploma in Muslim Chaplaincy. The Zaytuna Institute in Hayward, California, is also developing a full-time seminary. The Institute of Ismaili Studies in London has been training *waezeen* and religious education teachers for the world-wide Ismaili community, including that living in Canada. These institutions are deliberately positioning themselves as distinct from traditional religious schools. For example, London's Muslim College's "aims and objectives" include the following:

> Students of the Muslim College are expected to develop a critical approach to traditional and contemporary issues of religion, and to combine theoretical, vocational and practical experiences in their evaluation of the religiously plural situation.
>
> They are to develop an appreciation of the challenges that modern life poses to Islam and religion in general, and the impact that the interaction between Islam and modernity leaves on the patterns of culture, belief and social behaviour. (The Muslim College, 2005)

Praxis

A key characteristic of Islamic intellectual authority mentioned in the focus group discussions was the ability of the scholar or religious leader to deal with practical issues. This ranged from the perception of such a person addressing issues that were culturally relevant in Western contexts to being an activist. It included enabling Muslims to participate in society as citizens, endeavouring to establish Muslim institutions in the West, and carrying out charitable work.

There was a running thread in the Ottawa session on the involvement of scientists in contemporary Islamic discourse, which was seen by AK as being part of the historical tradition represented in the past by "Ibn Sina or Omar Khayyam, who were holistic." He mentioned the names of Hasan Fathi, a twentieth-century Egyptian architect; Abdus Salam, a Pakistani physicist and the first Muslim Nobel Prize winner; Pervez Hoodhboy, a Pakistani physicist and political writer; and Ziauddin Sardar, a British Muslim who has written on the history of science:

> they come from the scientific traditions, so there's an element of rationality. Because, whether you live in the West or the East, the law of gravity applies. So you cannot but be rational when you're pursuing science. So, that particular bent sort of gives them an insight when they're looking at the causes of why the Islamic society is ... or ... the struggles the Muslims are facing, and the consequences of their choices.

MT said in this discussion that one of his key role models was

> Hasan Fathi of Egypt, because I chose architecture as my profession and I was brought up by my parents to believe that you learn directly from people, you don't learn from books. You need the person. And, there's a saying by Rumi that "a moment in the presence of masters is worth more than a thousand years of worship," so to speak. So, right from an early age, I tried to find these people and be with them ... I left my study and went to Egypt to meet Hasan Fathi, and spent one month with him. And, what I learned from him was how you live the life of an intellectual, as a lived life ... So, when you're young and you see this embodiment in front

of you, it's an amazing moment. I think you learn by looking, really. So, here I had this example of an architect who was an important authority on architecture...

EL, in the Montreal session, was appreciative of the work of Mohammed Elmasry, an engineering professor who is the founder of the Canadian Islamic Congress, and whose work she described as "practical and theoretical sometimes... about how Muslims live in the West."

The coalescence of scientific pursuit, Islamic knowledge, and practice of religious faith appears to be a strong point of attraction for these interlocutors. But one did not have to be a full-fledged scientist to have insight into practical matters of pursing an Islamic way of life. In the Montreal discussion, OW, an eighteen-year old of European ethnicity, referred to several converts in the Bay area in California who had become imams: Hamza Yusuf, Zaid Shakir,[8] and Shuaib Webb. He related that

> these are people who ... pursued ... education in terms of Western sciences, and then pursued other types of education within the Islamic sciences. But still to a degree, especially the three of them, have sort of contact with a certain community and understanding of the problems and the pitfalls that people face, and how to try to navigate them ... There's this group in Chicago ... it's called ... IMAN [Inner-city Muslim Action Network]. And what they've done is ... a lot of projects where they do social work but they make social work sort of broad, and they just try and make an impact in a broad way, like without being overly ... didactic about Islamic themes or Islamic whatever ... [T]he concept is just that they're working ... within sort of the confines of the *Shariah*, but ... nonetheless not ... being overt and didactic about, [why] exactly ... we're doing this, because Islam says this or whatever ...

OW appeared to be appreciative of Muslim leaders who lead by example.

Some participants saw aspects of practicality in the work of certain academics. DO in the Ottawa discussion referred to Tariq Ramadan:

> The reason he impressed me so much is that he writes about being Muslim and living in the West. And he was born in the West and I grew up in the West, so when he talks about his own experience, I can actually relate to it. Being Muslim and growing up in a non-Muslim country is very hard. You're faced with a lot of challenges. And, he talks about how you can contribute to this society and still remain Muslim and remain true to your own beliefs.

The discussions touched on issues of confused identities among Muslims, especially the youth. There was greater confidence in Muslim scholars of Islam who were born or had lived in the West and were educated in Western universities than in traditionally trained imams to address these problems effectively.

Critical Approaches

Certain focus group respondents expressed an interest in critical approaches to understanding Muslim history and theology. The desired level of critical thinking varied from person to person. Several positions were staked out – from the need for debate to disagreeing with elements within scripture. Such dissent was seen as being very much part of the Muslim tradition despite the dominantly conservative Muslim discourses, which generally tend to abhor any criticism of the normative creed (see Abou El Fadl 2001 and Arkoun 2002).

A number of the participants indicated that while they were in their home countries they had accepted what they had learnt from religious teachers and parents about Islam at face value. However, upon living in the West they were exposed to other ways of thinking – by both Muslim and non-Muslim scholars. MN in Montreal said that Khaled Abou El Fadl "was the first to sort of open my mind to the fact that you can question things in Islam ... And, he was very clear in making distinctions between the Qur'an and *hadith* (the Prophet's traditions) as the basis for *Shariah*, Islamic law, and *fiqh* . . ." It appears that MN's traditional religious education had made him view scripture and "*Shariah*, Islamic law, and *fiqh*" as having the same theological value, which was later corrected through his reading of Abou El Fadl.

EH, a doctoral student of Muslim architecture in Montreal, espoused a particular critical perspective in which he saw a much larger conception of knowledge in the Islamic worldview than in the Western one.

> I think we as Muslims, we have the most widely open epistemology. Our epistemology encompasses different spectrums of human knowledge: what's wrong, what's right, how we can know things, and the veracity of things, how we establish the veracity of the things which we know . . . it's not only from [a] Muslim point of view but also through the critique of Muslim scholars who critique modernity, that modernity is a reductivist paradigm. So we have to realize that when we are living in Western society, that this culture doesn't account for many things which we hold to be necessary and actually [are] at the basis of our epistemology. This will create some kind of miscommunication, or like inability on our part to explain things, because our project is larger, the base on which we deal with reality is much larger. They have fewer colours in their spectrum . . .

Not only was the Western conception of modernity flawed, according to him, the very epistemological basis of Western knowledge was skewed. Conversely, a number of participants iterated that as Muslims they did not necessarily eschew Western knowledge, citing scripture to support this belief.

MK in Montreal was emphatic in his criticism of the lack of freedom of thought among Muslims currently: "there's no space for *ijtihad* [reasoning], or scepticism, or reading, or anything. And, that's maybe why I find that Christians have so much liberty in exploring the Muslim religion more than Muslim people do." In the same session, EL suggested the reasons why Muslim intellectuals were, in her opinion, unable to address pressing issues adequately:

some of them have been stuck in the boat [sic], and others are
... afraid from [sic] the public outcry against them if they
become progressives, so they want to please the majority, so
they can't move forward. Those who can, move forward –
some others can't move forward because of the way they have
been trained.

The travails of Muhammad Said al-Ashmawi and Nasr Hamid Abu Zaid, two Muslim intellectuals from Egypt who had openly espoused critical approaches, were cited in the discussions. MK in Montreal said that Abu Zaid

> tries to break the literalism of strict followers of the Qur'an and presents a different opinion. And, this person has been hassled big time. He was decreed an infidel in Egypt, making his marriage to his wife illegal, and he had to flee the country ...

FO stated in the same session that although she was secular in outlook, as a result of such persecution, "it's important for me, as a Muslim, to speak, and also to give voice to the kind of woman I am, and I have presented a kind of [inaudible], which is rationalistic." Despite having distanced herself from the practice of Islam, it became an issue of solidarity for her to identify with the rationalist approach of Muslim scholars who were seeking to examine the Islamic heritage with a critical perspective.

Two discussants in Montreal cited Irshad Manji, who calls herself a "Muslim refusenik" (2003), in response to the question of which Muslim intellectual had influenced them the most. EH said that "The existence of such writings and of looking at such logic and defining the flaws in it, and how each individual looks at it, helps as well to find your way." OW noted that

> despite the fact that I don't agree with much of what she says, I find Irshad Manji very interesting ... She's put into a book a lot of the problems that many Muslims have with Islam as a

body politic. I think, when it comes to her arguments about Islam in terms of fundamental issues, about historical issues, I think she's totally out of her league, and she doesn't know what she's talking about. But she does sort of have a common touch of what the issues of the body politic of Muslims is [sic] towards the way that mosques can be structured or certainly these other issues, and it's, if you want a sense of what that problem is, and I've been talking to people over and over again, you hear the same things that she's sort of enunciating. You get that same sentiment from her. She's sort of put it down. She's sort of an Everywoman...

Such willingness to look at the observations of a writer who has vigorously criticized established Muslim structures and values seems to indicate the existence of an openness to the multiple discourses on contemporary Islamic practice.

A number of discussants in Ottawa addressed the existence in Muslim history of open critical approaches to the pursuit of knowledge. MT referred to

the debate between Ibn Rushd and Ibn Ghazali [sic]... These two people were the intellectuals of the world at this time; not the Muslim world, of the [entire] world... and they're beating the daylights out of each other, disagreeing completely with each other, and they're refuting each other's claims.

This appeared to be in stark contrast to the perceived poverty of debate among contemporary Muslims on religious issues. DO said that

when I compare... our state of knowledge now... to what we had 400 years back, I think that we [have] kind of regressed. Because, back in the day, they used to challenge one another. And, if you came up with some new idea, people weren't afraid of that. You could talk about it.

A number of interlocutors commented on the widespread tendency for Muslims to have a binary approach to religious matters. There was perceived to be a resistance towards examining the finer details of an issue. Several discussants complained that Muslims were not living up to the rhetoric of engaging in serious debate.

SMF in Ottawa, on the other hand, was not certain about the veracity of the *hadith*, the Prophet's traditions. He also emphasized the Qur'an's allegorical language, which, according to him, has led to the selective adherence of its guidance by Muslims.

> In Pickthall's translation, verse 27 [of the Chapter of The Troops] reads: "And verily We have coined for mankind in this Qur'an all kinds of similitudes, that haply they may reflect." So, the Qur'an already has given us all the loopholes, or all the freedom, that is reflected . . . according to circumstances. Definitely, everything that happened during Muhammad's time is not final. There are so many things; that's why the Qur'an has already covered that issue, but we, the Muslims, we do pick and choose places . . . So, it's not the Qur'an that's in the problem, it's our interpretation of the Qur'an. Second, the word *sunna* [the practice of the Prophet], as we believe [it]. Qur'an has many times . . . said, "Obey Allah and obey the Prophet." It never says "obey Allah and *follow* the Prophet" . . . So that doesn't mean that we have to follow Muhammad the way he picked up [sic] his hair or moustache. This is not what Qur'an actually meant. This is obey, that means the judgment given by him has to be obeyed, or the order given by him in the courts has to be obeyed. That's what Qur'an says . . . I feel, that we have misinterpreted Qur'an, we have misinterpreted the term *sunna* and that's why we are bogged down with the problems of the world, what to do with transplantation . . . Secondly, *hadiths* was [sic] created 200 years after the . . . death of Prophet Muhammad. 200 years! So obviously nobody can trace what was told by Muhammad at that time . . . [yet] that is central to . . . our religion . . .

He seems to be suggesting that Muslims have significant leeway in the way they choose to live their lives and this does not need to be regulated by the Prophet's example. Consequently, answers to issues of organ transplantation and other bio-ethical matters do not have to be sought in the *hadith*. This view is not part of the dominant discourses of Muslims, but certainly appears present in contemporary debates among them. It is indicative of the intellectual challenge to normative modes within Islam.

Conclusion

The sociological conditions that exist presently for Muslims in the West are historically unique. Not only do they have unprecedented physical access to sources in printed and electronic forms, they also have knowledge of Western languages in which a significant amount of material on Islam is published. In previous times, a lack of knowledge of the major Muslim languages, especially Arabic, hampered participation in Islamic discourses among the non-Arabic speakers who formed the majority of Muslims. Interlocutors in the focus groups mentioned that certain English translations of Islamic scripture were the most important literature in their understanding of Islam. They confidently participated in the discussions, quoting chapter and verse in English. Topics that had previously been limited to the purview of intellectual elites have become part of the religious debates among a larger number of Muslims.

This research indicates that the emergent criteria for Islamic religious authority include knowledge of Western cultural context, praxis and critical thinking. Several discussants indicated that their regard for those who had traditionally been held as Islamic intellectual authorities had declined, if it had not vanished altogether. They were still willing to listen to certain figures, but not with blind faith. They expected scholars, in addition to having a substantial knowledge of Islamic sources, to be cognizant of the Canadian conditions in which Muslim communities live and to demonstrate a certain practicality based on their Islamic beliefs. Increasingly, the believers appear to be insisting on thinking for themselves and utilizing their rationality when approaching personal matters of faith. Exposure to contemporary Western approaches to the examination of texts has reintroduced into Muslim discourses a criticality that had all but disappeared in the recent past.[9] The well-read faithful are beginning to examine for themselves the theological status of scripture and religious law and their pertinence to the regulation of their religious and social lives.

The issues under debate also reach out into broader socio-political discussions of the societies in which they live. Muslim individuals are looking at their roles as citizens of Western countries together with the concepts of being good Muslims. Such thought has significant implications in contemporary times when the followers of Islam are facing a range of social options that include assimilation into secularism, at one end, and embracing religious extremism, at another. A number of interlocutors mentioned the importance that they gave to living balanced lives. The solutions that Muslims in the West will choose will differ between communities and individuals; however, the discursive journeys towards these ends and their outcomes will necessarily have implications for society at large.

A Case of Mistaken Identity: Inside and Outside the Muslim Ummah

ANAR ALI

Where Are You From?

As an immigrant or person of colour, "Where are you from?" is a question – among a list of others like "What does your name mean?" – that you get used to from a very young age. My response, as a child new to this country, had been Nairobi. But Nairobi was not a city or even a name that many people recognized. This was Canada (and Alberta) circa 1979 – at the beginning of Trudeau's policy of multiculturalism, a dream to build a diverse and tolerant society. Over 30 years later, it is a question I still face regularly.

I soon learned that I would have to zoom out, as you would nowadays on a Google map. But when I offered "Kenya," more often than not, the quizzical looks would persist. I would, it seemed, have to zoom out further. My new response was either "East Africa" and more often than not, just "Africa." (It had never occurred to me to say "India" – India after all was a country that belonged to my grandparents, not me. This is a concept that came to bear recently when my six-year-old niece Hana asked me, "Why am *I* brown? I was born in Canada.")

The answer "Africa" satisfied my classmates and teachers immensely. They knew Africa – they could locate it on the map! To my surprise, they were thrilled to have an African amongst them. Throw in a last name like Mohamedali (which I grew up with until I shortened it to Ali) and all the pieces of the puzzle fell into place. They were convinced I was going to be their star athlete. Invitations to lunch, offers of candy, and seats on the school bus were saved for me. Somehow I understood – or just accepted – their confusion about my race. But what puzzled me was, Why had no one had noticed my scrawny frame and thick glasses? I waited nervously for them to find me out.

It did not take long. I remember the look of disgust on Reg Osborne's face – the class jock (and naturally the boy we all liked) – when he found me hiding behind a tree, bent over in pain, huffing and puffing, unable to complete the Turkey Trot, an annual race in which I was pegged to be one of the winners. Word spread quickly and before I could defend myself (I was sick. I ate a rotten sandwich at lunch. I had cramps.), my star status was stripped away. Eventually, I found my rightful place with the nerds.

To my classmates (and teachers) I was black, and possibly they considered all people of colour to be black. Certainly, brown equated to black and so they applied their stereotypes of black people on me.

Posts 9/11, Muslims (and brown or Middle Eastern-looking people) now face a similar problem of mistaken identities. A personal example: In 2004, I was detained for three hours en route from Calgary to Los Angeles when the South Asian Arts festival I was attending was suspected of being a radical Muslim group. The festival's name, Artwallah, is a play on words, a mix of the words "art" and "wallah." Wallah is a Hindi-derived word that denotes a profession; examples include taxi-wallah and chai-wallah. The presence of (w)Allah in the festival raised flags. It was only after a thorough investigation and phone calls to England to confirm the whereabouts of an "evil person" with a name similar to mine – "Ali," I reassured the officer, was akin to "Smith" – that I was finally released.

Islam is often treated as a monolithic entity rather than a pluralistic one. Islamic fundamentalism has come to represent all of Islam. Yet we do not, for instance, generalize about Catholics based on the Irish Republican Army, Christians based on the zealously patriotic Christian right in the United States, Jewish people based on Zionist fundamentalism, or Hindus based on the Bharatiya Janata Party.

Specificity demands effort and education. Edward Said calls it a clash of ignorance.

And there is nothing like *not knowing* to generate fear. It is akin, I think, to the intense fear that builds in horror films. When we cannot see the predator, when we do not know where he/it is, our fear increases. But once it appears on the screen, once we see it, somehow our fear dissipates.

The question then becomes why is there such overwhelming fear of Islam and Muslims when other communities, other religions rarely receive a similar response?

During an interview with *Spiegel International*, the Aga Khan, imam of Ismaili-Muslims, said it well. "You would think that an educated person in the twenty-first century should know something about Islam; but you look at education in the Western world and you see that Islamic civilizations have been absent. What is taught about Islam? As far as I know – nothing. What was known about Shiism before the Iranian revolution? What was known about the radical Sunni Wahhabism before the rise of the Taliban? We need a big educational effort to overcome this."[1]

It is easier to locate Africa on a world map than it is Nairobi.

Don't Speak for Me, Irshad Manji

Generalizations about Muslims persist – not just from outside the Ummah but from inside as well. Take Irshad Manji as an example. She claims to speak about mainstream Islam – the majority of Muslims – but she speaks about it as if they were a monolithic mass. In the first few pages of her book *The Trouble with Islam*, she names communities like the Soviet Jews (from whom she takes her stance as a Refusnik) or the Rose of Sharon Baptist Church, where she attended an after-school program.

But when she speaks about Muslims, she rarely gets specific – never naming her own community and often using the pronouns "us" and "we."

Yet even within a sect – as with other religions – there can be dramatically different interpretations – and for that matter, opinions.

Irshad Manji and I have similar backgrounds. We are the same age; we are both of Indian origin; my family is from Kenya and Tanzania, hers is from neighbouring Uganda; she grew up in Western Canada, so did I; the Shia Muslim communities we belong to are closely connected historically – a schism about the authority of the next rightful imam split the groups. Yet our experiences of Islam are drastically different. While Manji was plucked out of the Rose of Sharon Baptist Church after winning the Most Promising Christian of the Year, my father encouraged me to read the Bible when all the students in my Grade 4 class were each given a free copy. While women could not lead prayers at her madrassa, both women and men lead prayers at our jamatkhana. While she heard anti-Semitic rhetoric at the madrassa, I first learned about the Israeli-Palestinian conflict from an old Jewish man I sat next to on a plane from Calgary to Toronto. "You know," he said with a smile and then offered me a piece of gum, "we are not supposed to get along this well." While the imam of her madrassa insisted women were inferior, the imam of the Ismailis – the Aga Khan – advocates for women's rights and builds schools for girls in developing nations like Afghanistan.

My point is not that she should not voice her opinions, tell her stories, advocate for change but that we need to be more specific when we speak about Muslims – just as we are when we discuss other communities.

There are one billion Muslims in the world.

But Who Will Speak for Me?

My first book, *Baby Khaki's Wings*, is a collection of stories set in the East African Ismaili Muslim community. During the book tour, I was asked, on more than one occasion, by an Ismaili member of the audience, "But who gave you permission to write the book?" What a question! But I was not surprised. I understood the question.

Ismailis have a long history of upheaval and dislocation having been a stateless community for over 800 years. They have faced religious persecution for centuries, which has led to the practice of taqiyya or voluntary dissimulation. The key to self-preservation has been self-censorship, concealment, blending in, living without being detected.

Taqiyya is a centuries-old tradition, but it is still practised today. In countries like Afghanistan and Saudi Arabia, Ismailis still conceal their identity, pretending to be, most likely, Sunni Muslim. In the West, taqiyya expresses itself differently. While Ismailis are not a persecuted community here, there is still a fear about speaking out, of naming ourselves, engaging in anything that might make us vulnerable or appear controversial. It is akin to a vestigial trait – the appendix in humans or leg bones in whales – it is not needed anymore but is still part of our makeup.

I felt the power of this reflex (trait) intensely when my book was first published. I spent many sleepless nights worried about whether I had made the right decision to name the Ismailis instead of creating a fictional stand-in. The book is far from controversial but no one (as far as I knew) had directly named the community in modern fiction. In the end, I decided that it was imperative for me not to practice taqiyya in my writing. It became a political act to proclaim my identity, to name my community, and by extension to fully engage in the world rather than remain "underground."

Ismaili Muslims, even in the West, are not considered Muslim *enough* – "Muslims Lite" as comedian Russell Peters jokes. Tarek Fatah illustrates the point in an article published in the *Toronto Star*. "In the weeks leading up to the [2004 federal] election, many Muslim organizations published a list of Muslim candidates running for Parliament. Conspicuous by their absence on these lists were the names of Liberal Yasmin Ratansi and sitting Conservative MP Rahim Jaffer. They were ignored because they belong to the Ismaili sect of Islam and thus are not considered worthy of the label Muslim." He goes on to add. "In their search for genuine Muslims who carried credentials of authenticity by the conservative (Muslim) leadership, the media overlooked Ms Ratansi, and failed to give her the credit she so rightly deserves as a torchbearer for Muslims in Canada."[2]

This puts Ismailis between the proverbial rock and a hard place. Outside the Ummah, they are part of the monolithic Muslim identity, yet inside they are often excluded – reinforcing old feelings of persecution and the subsequent reluctance to speak out.

Yet Ismailis, given their long history of dislocation, often straddle multiple worlds – in my case India-Tanzania-Kenya-Ismaili-Muslim-Canada-Alberta – and therefore offer a unique perspective. They are simultaneously insiders and outsiders in several communities. At a time of increasingly intractable and dangerous conflicts in our divided world, the voices of people with the ability to see from many points of view might prove extremely useful.

A Yoruba myth illustrates this point poignantly. One day, Eshu, the trickster-god, walked down the road, wearing a hat. "Did you notice the fellow in the red hat?" a farmer asked his neighbour and friend who lived on the other side of the road. "No. I did see a fellow pass by but his hat was blue." "You're wrong," insisted the first. "You're wrong," retorted the second. Soon, the entire village was involved, each arguing adamantly about the colour of the hat. Eshu returned just in time to show the villagers how easily they were fooled and to teach them the importance of perspective. His hat was blue on one side and red on the other. From one side of the road, only the blue side had been visible, from the other, only the red half. (In many versions of this tale, Eshu does not stop the fighting and soon the villagers destroy each other.)

More Ismailis will, I hope, offer their opinions, share their thoughts, and write their stories. It would, ironically, also help dissipate our nervousness and fear.

Pakistani poet Faiz Ahmed Faiz puts it eloquently.

Speak – your lips are free.
Speak – your tongue is still yours.
This magnificent body
Is still yours.

. . .

Speak – there is little time
But little though it is
It is enough.
Time enough
Before the body perishes –
Before the tongue atrophies.
Speak – truth still lives.
Say what you have
To say.[3]

Victim or Aggressor?
Typecasting Muslim Women for Their Attire

NATASHA BAKHT

Debates about the attire of Muslim women have been flooding the editorial pages of newspapers the world over. Several countries have seen controversies about the way some Muslim women dress. Whether it is the banning of headscarves in French schools, the dismissal of a Swiss schoolteacher for wearing a hijab,[1] a challenge brought by the defence in a New Zealand car theft case where a Muslim witness chose to give evidence wearing a niqab,[2] the expulsion of a hijab-wearing Turkish student from medical school,[3] or the dismissal of an American woman's small claims dispute for refusing to remove her full-face veil;[4] it seems that the public, media and governments cannot get enough of scrutinizing and indeed penalizing Muslim women for what they wear. It appears that many people have an opinion about how Muslim women ought to dress, including some Muslims themselves who offer definitive answers to contentious issues by attempting to rely on "authentic religious requirements." Despite the fact that both Muslim and non-Muslim women have been concealing parts of their bodies for centuries, this topic seems far from reaching the public's saturation point. This essay examines Canadian case studies where Muslim women are prevented from participating in some activity because of their head or face coverings. The justifications for banning Muslim women from these activities reveal a tension between the need to protect Muslim women and the need to be protected from them.

Protecting Muslim Women from the Dangers of the Hijab

Perhaps the most commonly heard opposition to the veil is that women cover their faces or heads at the command of domineering men, so that the veil is seen as a sign of Muslim women's oppression, as well as a general indicator of the "backwardness" of Islamic culture. Sherene Razack has argued that three stereotypical figures, "the 'imperiled' Muslim woman, the 'dangerous' Muslim man and the 'civilized' European,'" repeatedly reappear in the Western imaginary to justify the expulsion of Muslims from the political community.[5] The idea that Muslim women who wear the hijab must be rescued from the confines of their community is pervasive indeed.[6]

More recently, a novel version of the need to protect veiled women has emerged in the Canadian debate. As more and more Muslim women are vocal about their choice to don the hijab and because these women are pursuing higher education, teaching in schools, running for political office, and advocating in courts of law, it is no longer possible to easily fit them into the stereotypical box of the "imperilled" Muslim woman. Rather than protecting women from "dangerous Muslim men" or the symbolic assault that the hijab represents to women's equality, we must now step in to protect Muslim women from the dangers of the physical headscarf itself!

Recently, a young hijab-wearing woman in Quebec, Sondos Abdelatif, who had completed her initial examinations and was enrolled in a prison guard training course, was told that she could not become a prison guard unless she removed her hijab. The argument supporting the ban was based on the contention that her headscarf could be used against her as a strangulation device. Sarah Elgazzar, a spokesperson for the Canadian Council on American Islamic Relations stated, "If there were security concerns they should have addressed the security concerns." Elgazzar noted that there are specifically designed hijabs used by the Canadian armed forces that could have been used as a compromise in this situation. But a spokesperson from the Public Safety Department said no alternatives to the ultimatum were being considered.[7]

Similarly, an eleven-year-old Ottawa girl was ejected from a soccer game in Quebec after she refused to remove her headscarf during the game. The referee claimed that removing the hijab was necessary as a safety precaution. The Quebec Soccer Association's spokesperson pointed out "that the referee is Muslim himself [to demonstrate that the decision was not discriminatory], and that the ban on hijabs is to protect children from being accidentally strangled."[8] Although five young teams from across Canada walked out of a Quebec soccer tournament as a result of the ban, the Fédération Internationale de Football Association, or FIFA, upheld the referee's decision and remained firm in their intention not to change the regulations – or explain them.[9]

The FIFA rules do not explicitly ban the hijab, they simply give discretion to a referee to determine whether a headscarf is safe to wear. Mohamed El Rashidy, the director of the Canadian Arab Federation, has noted that "[t]he status quo in soccer games has been to allow female players to wear the hijab."[10] But this is apparently changing. The FIFA ruling undermines attempts to build bridges between Muslim minorities and the wider society. It also sends the demeaning message to Muslim women and girls, mostly of South Asian descent, that soccer is not for them. Joe Guest, the Canadian Soccer Association's chief referee, has pointed to the incongruity of the FIFA ruling, stating that it seems to indicate that "players can't wear prescription eye-glasses. But they do."[11]

In the same vein, five girls were barred from taking part in a taekwondo tournament in Longueuil, Quebec because they wore the hijab. Organizers of Quebec's Taekwondo Federation said the sport's rules prevent women from competing in hijab despite the fact that youth and women have taken part in tournaments both provincially and internationally for more than five years.[12] The World Taekwondo Federation (WTF) sanctioned this decision. Thus, Muslim women who participate in competitions endorsed by the WTF will no longer be permitted to wear a hijab. Because the WTF is recognized by the International Olympic Committee, this ruling will also have an impact on Muslim women's ability to compete in the Olympic summer games in Beijing in 2008.[13]

The decisions to exclude Muslim women from sport, often taken by federations comprised of all male and non-Muslim people, strike at the heart of religious freedom. "It seems that Muslim women now have to make a choice between their faith and sport."[14] Rulings such as the FIFA one that preserve the discretionary powers of referees to exclude headscarves only perpetuate the uncertainty that Muslim women or girls must cope with, never knowing until the last minute whether they will be ejected from a game or tournament despite months of training and hard work. Thus Muslim girls and women are at the mercy of individuals who may or may not allow them to participate in sporting activities. Real safety issues can and should be dealt with legitimately. But sports officials have never pointed to a single incident when the wearing of a hijab has endangered any player. The creation of "sport hijabs" that can come off easily because of a Velcro strap tied at the back of the neck have already been created and worn by Muslim girls as a compromise to assuage safety concerns.[15] Unfortunately, there appear to be few concessions from sports officials despite serious concerns about the violation of fundamental rights.

The need to rescue Muslim women from the dangers of a scarf is indicative of an attitude of superiority. That these feeble, ignorant, young creatures would not know what is good for them or how to save themselves from harm is of course a typically racist position grounded in the desire to "civilize" a group of people. The harm caused to such women is not the remote harm of being strangled by a headscarf but the steadfast commitment to exclude them from public life.

Protecting Canadians from Fraudulent Muslim Women

We have barely dealt with the fact that some Muslim women wear the hijab when the latest focus of anti-Muslim hysteria, this time over women who wear the niqab, is in full swing. In October 2006, comments made by the leader of the British House of Commons, Jack Straw, sparked massive controversy about Muslim women who wear the full-face veil with narrow slits for the eyes. Mr Straw asked Muslim women meeting with him to remove the niqab, stressing *his* discomfort in interacting with niqab-wearing women and arguing that the niqab "set the wearer apart"[16] and acted as "a visible statement of separation and difference."[17] Former British Prime Minister Tony

Blair joined in the contentious debate, indicating that the niqab makes "other people from outside the community feel uncomfortable."[18]

Canada has not been immune to the growing agitation that has been expressed about Muslim women who cover their faces. Although there has been no overt declaration to try to ban women who wear the niqab in public spaces as in other countries,[19] Canadian politicians have relied on other not-so-subtle means of disciplining Muslim women who defy social conventions of dress.

In a recent Quebec provincial election campaign, a controversy was sparked when it was announced that electoral officers would *not* require a niqab-wearing woman to lift her veil to identify herself to vote. The chief electoral officer noted that the permission to wear the niqab and vote was not religious accommodation, but rather the application of a general rule that if someone comes to vote without identification, the person can make a sworn statement or have another person vouch for his or her identity. André Boislair, leader of the Parti Quebecois, argued that the "exception" for veiled women was completely unacceptable, and that if he was elected premier he would have the electoral law amended.[20]

Facing political pressure, and even threatening phone calls, Marcel Blanchet, the chief electoral officer reversed his earlier decision and made it obligatory for women to remove their full-face veils in order to vote. Elections Quebec justified this reversal of policy by stating that they were concerned that unrest would occur at the polls and that some non-Muslim citizens had threatened to wear Halloween masks at polling stations.[21]

This veiled-voting incident in Quebec was followed in Canada with the introduction of Bill C-6, *An Act to amend the Canada Elections Act (visual identification of voters)*. The bill, which was introduced by the Conservative government, requires that voters who present identification in order to (1) vote, (2) register to vote, or (3) vouch for another voter must have their faces uncovered to enable election officials to identify them visually. The bill is apparently an attempt to prevent voter fraud, although as pointed out by several opposition MPs, little evidence of a problem of voter fraud exists in Canada.[22]

Interestingly, in response to media questions, the chief electoral officer of Canada, Marc Mayrand, had the same initial reaction to veiled-voting as the Quebec chief electoral officer. He indicated that he would not require women who wear niqabs or burqas to remove their face coverings in order to vote. He noted that because voters are offered two alternatives to voting without photo identification (i.e. providing two pieces of non-photo ID or taking an oath), an uncovered face could not be a requirement under the *Canada Elections Act*[23] since there would be no means of taking a visual comparison of the voter's face with a photograph. He also noted that the Act provides for other means of voting that do not require the visual comparison of a voter with her photograph, such as voting by mail.[24]

Despite these inconsistencies, Canadian politicians have insisted that showing one's face in order to vote is necessary for identification purposes. Prime Minister Stephen Harper while on a visit to Australia stated, "I profoundly disagree with the decision [of Marc Mayrand]"[25] but failed to provide any explanation for the contradictory requirements in the Act. Thus, a niqab-wearing woman could, under the new Act, be forced to remove her veil at a polling station despite elections officials being unable to visually identify her because she has chosen to present two pieces of non-photo identification that recognize her name and her address, as per the requirements of the *Canada Elections Act*.

This illogical reasoning strongly suggests that the only reason for the amendment to the Act is to target an already besieged and vulnerable minority group. "This is not about safety, not about security, not about fraud, it's about targeting a community that is seen as dangerous ... [and] criminal."[26] As one *Globe and Mail* editorial pointed out, showing one's face would only prove that the voter "has a face."[27]

The reasoning proposed by the government on this issue defies logic. Why have such a small group of women, indeed already marginalized from mainstream society, provoked such a rash response from the highest levels of our political community? If many people can vote in Canada without having to be visually identified, the only reason to insist on visually identifying some Muslim women for voting purposes is mistrust. Clearly, the government, with its relentless emphasis on the unsubstantiated claim of fraud and the requirement of identification, simply does not have faith in Muslim women.

Unhelpful Muslim Responses: Religious Requirements

Many Muslim women who do not cover their heads or faces use religious arguments to oppose the wearing of the niqab. Raheel Raza has stated: "Contrary to some peoples view [sic], covering the face is not a religious requirement for Muslim women."[28] In response to a British Muslim woman who lost her job because she wore the full-face veil, Farzana Hassan, president of the Muslim Canadian Congress, stated "There is nothing specified in the Qur'an that says you need to cover your face . . . The veil is a tradition, a tool of oppression created by men."[29] They claim in their defence that a very small percentage of Muslim women choose to cover their faces.

There appears to be little willingness on the part of these Muslims to accept, firstly, that different women may adhere to different levels of religiousity, and, secondly, that there may simply be a difference of opinion amongst Muslims about religious requirements. Muslims are made up of people from a vast assortment of races, countries of origin, and beliefs. Diversities are so pronounced in this amorphous, divergent, and shifting composition of individuals and groups that it is not uncommon to come across Muslims who are in conflict with one another.

Discerning the significance of religious requirements is not easy. Courts, which are typically in the business of assessing evidence to make factual determinations, have recognized the futility in evaluating religious requirements. The Supreme Court of Canada has devised a test of religious belief in which an individual's sincere conviction is given predominance over even the normative belief purported by religious authorities or the religious community in question.[30] Such a limited legal test is necessary to protect the convictions of individuals who may dissent from the mainstream views of their religious community. It also sustains the idea that faith, even within a single belief system, will have multiple and mutable interpretations.

Conclusion: Contradictory Stereotypes

What is interesting about the hijab and niqab debates in the aforementioned case studies is the seemingly contradictory views of Muslim women and girls that are projected.[31] Like most stereotypes, there is little evidence to suggest that either typecast is accurate or reflective of the lives of Muslim women.

The first typecast is drawn from the ubiquitous belief that Muslim women are victims. These "imperiled Muslim women" are victims of a gender oppressive religion. They are in need of protection from "dangerous Muslim men," and "civilized Europeans" are the ideal group to rescue these passive women and girls who are unable to help themselves. In the context of the women and girls who wear the hijab during certain employment and sports activities, this argument is modified, and the banning of the headscarf is justified to protect them from the dangers of the scarf itself which may unwittingly strangle them. Muslim women and girls are thus kept in a position of victimhood. They are prevented from taking their rightful place as active participants in society under the guise of guarding their safety.

The second typecast is that of the aggressor – a viewpoint that has become particularly popular in the post-9/11 era and has justified the surveillance and control of Muslim communities globally. The suspicious Muslim woman covers her face possibly to defraud the Canadian electoral system. Society must be protected from these dangerous destabilizers of the state who threaten to undermine the proper workings of the political system. Although other Canadians need not show their faces in order to vote, these particular Canadians cannot be trusted.

These two stereotypes are deployed in regards to the same group of women with no recognition of the conflict between the two images. On the one hand, Muslim women are victims who need to be protected from the dangerous practice of wearing a headscarf which could inadvertently choke them. On the other hand, Muslim women are a distrustful and dodgy group from whom Canadian society needs protection lest they defraud our political system. Both these stereotypes are equally and readily accessible in Canadian popular political culture.

Decisions to limit head and face coverings must be subject to rigorous rationalization. Otherwise, the decisions of sports officials, politicians, and others to ban hijabs and niqabs will simply serve to further marginalize Muslim women who wish to participate in public life and athletic activity. Creating solutions to those situations when legitimate safety or identification issues are at stake is usually quite simple. These solutions however, do not involve making declarations about the "correct" religious interpretation of modes of attire. Rather, one must respect women's agency regarding choice of dress and accommodate their needs generously. When the opposition to Muslim women's attire is irrational, like the knee-jerk responses to difference illustrated in this chapter, one must ask what is really going on. Sadly, honest dialogue has been absent from these debates and decisions have been rendered and buttressed without any appreciation of the actual issues.

Politics Over Principles: The Case of Omar Khadr

SHEEMA KHAN

The saga of Omar Khadr has yet to reach a conclusive end. Yet the tortuous journey of this young man will continue to have reverberations in many ways for years to come – in the fields of law, human rights, politics and, more importantly, what his case has to say about the value of Canadian citizenship.

While successive Federal regimes have acquiesced to the gulag that is Guantanamo Bay, public disclosure of Omar's plight has moved both our courts and the wider public to demand just treatment of a fellow human being. The fact that the Canadian government has failed to stand up for the human rights of one of its citizens – a Muslim – has not been lost on the nation's Muslim population.

The treatment of Omar Khadr follows a disturbing pattern of human rights abuses of Muslims in Canada in the wake of the terrorist attacks on American soil in 2001. These include government complicity with the notorious American practice of extraordinary rendition (Maher Arar); collusion with foreign security services in the detention and torture of Canadians travelling abroad (Abdullah Almalki, Ahmad El Maati and Muayyed Nureddin); and the use of secret evidence to detain immigrants (Hassan Almrei, Adil Charkaoui, Mohamed Harkat, Mahmoud Jaballah and Mohamed Zeki Mahjoub).

In the spring of 2008, Canadians learned of the case of Abousfian Abdelrazik, a forty-six-year-old Canadian of Sudanese origin who had been stranded in Sudan for nearly five years as successive Canadian governments thwarted efforts to bring him home to his family in

Montreal. According to federal government documents, he had been imprisoned in Khartoum at our own government's request. When he was eventually released, the government denied him a passport to return home to Canada. While the Harper government accuses him of links to al-Qaeda, he has never been charged with any crime. In trying to find an explanation for why the government won't bring him home, Mr Abdelrazik told the *Globe and Mail* on Canada Day in 2008 that "The Canadian government has a racist mind. It is because I am black and Muslim."[1] In addition, government documents from April 2008 reveal that fear of displeasing the Bush administration has played a significant role in its refusal to return Mr Abdelrazik to Canada: "Senior government of Canada officials should be mindful of the potential reaction of our US counterparts to Abdelrazik's return to Canada as he is on the US no-fly list . . . Continued cooperation between Canada and the US in the matters of security is essential. We will need to continue to work closely on issues related to the Security of North America, including the case of Mr Abdelrazik."[2]

The now infamous case of Maher Arar was the subject of an in-depth inquiry by Justice Dennis O'Connor that resulted in a multi-million dollar payout for Mr Arar from the Canadian government, and a slew of recommended changes to RCMP and CSIS practices (many of these recommendations remain unfulfilled two years and counting).

Much of the Iacobucci inquiry into the events surrounding the detention and torture of Almalki, El Maati, and Nureddin has been held behind closed doors. The findings, published in October 2008, vindicated the three Muslim men at the heart of the inquiry. Nonetheless, the government admitted in January 2008 that Canada was justified in working with countries accused of engaging in torture, saying that the United Nations *Convention Against Torture* was not a factor in deciding whether to send information to countries such as Syria and Egypt about Canadians detained there. However, as author Erna Paris notes, signatories to the UN *Convention Against Torture* (which includes Canada) are prohibited from transporting any individual to a country that practises torture.

Finally, the Supreme Court of Canada deemed portions of the security certificate legislation unconstitutional. Now, those held under a security certificate will have the right to security-cleared counsel who will have access to the evidence against the accused. The new process will still involve some court hearings that the suspects will not be permitted to attend.

These examples of injustice towards Canadian Muslims suggest that in a post-9/11 era, political, and security considerations take precedence over basic human rights. However, Canadian courts and human rights NGOs play an invaluable role in serving as bulwarks against government abuses of the *Canadian Charter*. It is this essential tension – between politics and principles – that serves as a backdrop for the unfolding drama of Omar Khadr.

Whether Omar Khadr remains in Guantanamo or is brought back to face trial here in Canada, there will be further examination of Canada's role in the "war on terror" and its adherence to international laws and norms.

The "Khadr Effect"

In order to discuss the predicament of Omar Khadr in proper context, one must first look at the history of the Khadr family and the incidents leading to Omar Khadr's detention. Michelle Shephard, author of *Guantanamo's Child: The Untold Story of Omar Khadr*, provides an excellent in-depth analysis of Omar's story.[3]

The family patriarch was Ahmed Said Khadr, an engineer, who moved to Canada from Egypt in 1977, and shortly thereafter married an Egyptian Palestinian refugee, Maha Elsamnah. In 1985, at the height of the Soviet occupation of Afghanistan, the family moved to Peshawar, Pakistan, where Mr Khadr was put in charge of the office of Human Concern International (HCI), an Ottawa-based charity that provided relief to Afghan refugees. Mr Khadr shuttled between Pakistan and Canada. Then, in 1995, Pakistani police charged Mr Khadr in connection with the bombing of the Egyptian embassy in Islamabad and imprisoned him. Protesting his innocence, Mr Khadr went on a hunger strike and was hospitalized. During that very period, then Prime Minister Jean Chrétien was on a state visit to Pakistan. Ms Elsamnah used the occasion to plead with the PM to secure her husband's release. During talks with then Pakistani PM Benazir Bhutto, Prime Minister Chrétien asked that Mr Khadr be treated fairly. A few weeks later, the charges were dropped and Mr Khadr was released. Subsequently, HCI fired Mr Khadr, who went on to run his own relief organization.

By 1998, Pakistani security agencies were after Mr Khadr again for alleged ties with Osama Bin Laden. The Khadr household – consisting of the parents and six children – were based in Jalalabad, Afghanistan. According to accounts provided by Zaynab Khadr in Lawrence Wright's "The Looming Towers," the Khadr clan shared a large family compound with the Bin Ladens in Jalalabad. Following 9/11, Ahmed Said Khadr's name was placed on an international list of terror suspects.

Chrétien's intervention in Khadr's case, and the subsequent link to Bin Laden, would later be known as the "Khadr effect" in Ottawa, and would play a significant role in the handling of Omar Khadr's affairs by both the Liberal and Conservative governments. Basically, this moniker signified the risk of prime ministerial intervention on behalf of those accused of terrorism.

It should be understood that all the Khadr children had been indoctrinated with the al-Qaeda ideology from an early age.

Omar's Story: Paying for the Sins of His Family

Born in Ontario, Omar Khadr moved with his family to Afghanistan permanently when he was 11 years of age. It was on July 27, 2002 that Omar Khadr, aged 15, was seriously wounded in a firefight with US soldiers in Afghanistan. He was accused of killing a medic, US Sergeant Christopher James Speer, during that fight, and was detained at the notorious Bagram Air Base for two months. One of his interrogators at Bagram prison was later courtmartialled for brutality and for the murder of a prisoner. Foreign Affairs was notified of the arrest on August 20. Even then, the government had concerns about the possible transfer of Omar to Guantanamo Bay; Canadian officials asked that Omar's age be taken into account. However, Stephen Harper, then head of the Canadian Alliance Party, told the media that his immediate concern was not that the fifteen-year-old be returned to Canada. Rather, the Canadian Alliance was more preoccupied "about Canada being a platform for activities that are dangerous to the Western Alliance."[4]

In late October, Omar was transferred to Guantanamo Bay. He was not permitted to see a lawyer and was subject to torture by American authorities. A few months later, in February 2003, Foreign Affairs announced that Canadian officials met with Omar, and that "he seem[ed] well."[5] As Canadians later learned, this meeting actually consisted of an interrogation by a CSIS official after Omar had been "softened up" by sleep deprivation techniques applied by the Americans. The video of fifteen-year-old Omar did not show that the teen seemed "well," but rather, that he was in obvious mental and physical distress. But this was not the first time that the Canadian government would be disingenuous about the state of Omar Khadr.

By the spring of 2004, the governments of Australia and Britain were actively trying to have their nationals removed from Guantanamo. Yet the Canadian government remained silent regarding the status of Omar Khadr. Dennis Edney, a Winnipeg-based lawyer, decided to act on behalf of Omar since Ottawa would not do so. He filed a legal brief challenging the legality of Omar's detention since he had been denied access to a lawyer for more than one and a half years, and underlined the importance of protecting children's rights.

Any hope of garnering public sympathy for Omar's plight were soon sabotaged by a controversial interview given by Omar's mother (Maha Elsamnah) and sister (Zaynab Khadr) to the CBC. Both women lambasted Canadian liberalism, its societal mores, and boasted of their friendship with Osama Bin Laden, as they prepared to use the Canadian health care system for the rehabilitation of the youngest Khadr child, Karim, shot in the back outside the home where his father, Ahmad Said Khadr, had been killed during combat. The response by Canadians was swift; almost 10,000 people signed an on-line petition demanding that the family be expelled from the country, while MP Stockwell Day suggested that they be barred from returning to Canada and a Liberal MP demanded that Ms Elsamnah be charged under the *Anti-terrorism Act*.

Given the huge unpopularity of the Khadr name, very few politicians dared to speak up on behalf of Omar Khadr, who was essentially paying the price for the sins of his family. According to three former Guantanamo Bay detainees Omar was "in constant pain" and was prevented from getting proper medical treatment – in direct contradiction to statements given by Canadian government officials. Yet in 2004 the story remained under the radar screen for most Canadians, due in part to the unpopularity of the Khadr family.

Meanwhile, Canadian intelligence agents continued to travel to Guantanamo to interrogate Omar, while he remained in the legal black hole of Guantanamo where he had no impartial tribunal before which he could either clear his name or be given a defined punishment. Nor could Omar argue that as a minor, he bore a diminished responsibility for his actions. Canada's domestic spy agency, CSIS, took full advantage of the situation to gather information that was then passed on to both the RCMP and American authorities. Canadian government authorities, unlike their British and Australian counterparts, did not press the American administration for due process. The best that Foreign Affairs Minister Pierre Pettigrew could muster was to unsuccessfully seek reassurances from the US that Omar would not be executed. The timidity and complicity of the Liberal government was shameful. Thankfully, the Canadian judicial system would not let politics get in the way of justice. In August 2005, the Federal Court ordered a temporary stop to these interrogations, pending a fuller hearing of Mr Khadr's *Charter* rights as a Canadian.

Calls for Justice

By early 2006, a chorus of world leaders had voiced unanimous objection to the existence of the military tribunals at Guantanamo Bay. A damning UN report found the prison falling far short of meeting international standards of justice, prompting British, French, German, and Italian leaders to demand the closing of Guantanamo. Not only did Canada remain conspicuously silent, but it went so far as to justify the need for Guantanamo – in step with the views of Donald Rumsfeld. While the Liberals had maintained a shameful silence, the new Conservative government unabashedly towed the

Bush administration's line. In fact, at the time, Canada's special-forces units in Afghanistan continued to hand terrorism suspects over to US forces who shipped at least some of them to Guantanamo.

Two years after arriving at Guantanamo, Omar Khadr finally had access to a lawyer, Muneer Ahmad. After the publication of the UN Report, Mr Ahmad criticized Ottawa for failing to stand up for the human rights of one of its citizens – a minor – while other Western allies had successfully lobbied the Bush administration to have their nationals returned. A year later, Omar was permitted to call his family – almost five years after arriving at Guantanamo.

While it seemed that Omar's case was on the verge of fading into oblivion, six former Canadian foreign ministers wrote an open letter to Prime Minister Harper on February 1, 2007 (the fifth anniversary of Guantanamo) to take action and demand that Guantanamo be closed down. Arguing that the detention centre "flagrantly violates human rights, undermines the rule of law, and sends a signal to other governments that it is acceptable to abuse the rights of their citizens,"[6] Joe Clark, Lloyd Axworthy, Flora MacDonald, Bill Graham, John Manley, and Pierre Pettigrew demanded that Harper press Washington to release the detainees immediately, unless they are to be charged and tried under recognized international standards of justice; not send the detainees to countries where they may face human-rights abuses; ensure that the ill-treatment and torture of the detainees stop immediately; forbid the use of evidence obtained under torture or ill-treatment and permit UN and other international human-rights experts full and private access to the detainees.

However, even this call did not move the Conservative government. Its silence remained inexplicable, even contradictory, to a statement made one week earlier by Prime Minister Harper after the settlement of the Arar affair: "Canada fully understands and appreciates and shares the United States' concerns with regard to security . . . However, the Canadian government has every right to go to bat when it believes one of its citizens has been treated unfairly by another government."[7] Taking this statement at face value, in combination with the inaction on the Khadr file, implies that the Canadian government either believes that Omar is being treated fairly by the US government (in spite of ample evidence to the contrary), or believes in a second-tiered citizenship for Omar.

Pressure mounted further still when Australia fought for and won the repatriation of one of its nationals, David Hicks, who struck a plea bargain and returned to Australia to serve nine months. Furthermore, as Omar's lawyer, Muneer Ahmad, pointed out, Omar is the first juvenile in modern history charged with war crimes; people of that age were not charged in Rwanda, Sierra Leone, or in the former Yugoslavia. When the military commission at Guantanamo dismissed the charges against Omar in June 2007 (on a technicality), the Canadian government could have lobbied to repatriate Omar, especially in face of the Kafka-like scenario where the US government promised to appeal the decision to an appeals court that had yet to be created. From the get-go, the American administration was making up the rules on the fly and Canadian officials were shirking their responsibilities towards a citizen.

The Canadian legal community began to find its voice after four years of silence. University of Ottawa associate professor and scholar of international law, Craig Forcese, supported the call for Mr Khadr's release, saying the twenty-year-old's detention has no basis in international law. At its annual convention in August 2007, the Canadian Bar Association (CBA) announced that it would pressure the federal government for Omar's release. Members of the CBA were moved to action after hearing the US military lawyer assigned to represent Mr Khadr – Lieutenant-Commander William Kuebler – speak about the travesty of justice in Guantanamo, and the deteriorating mental condition of Omar. In trying to explain the reason for government silence, lawyer Lorne Waldman (one of Maher Arar's lawyers) pointed to the infamous "Khadr effect" – that the media and the government shied away from speaking on behalf of Omar due to his family's notorious links to al-Qaeda. In fact, the *Globe and Mail* reported that then Foreign Affairs Minister Peter Mackay had scripted answers in response to possible media queries about the fate of Omar, which included deference to the highly flawed legal process.

Soon after the call by the CBA, legal experts began to question the feasibility of trying Omar in Canadian courts. The primary difficulty would lie in presenting evidence before the courts, and what evidence a Canadian judge would accept as untainted. For one, the Americans would have to agree to hand over their evidence, and courts would have to be satisfied that neither the Canadian nor US government was claiming too much secrecy. Also, lawyers for Omar could argue that self-incriminating statements ought to be inadmissible as he was physically abused and denied medical treatment. There is also the likelihood that Canadian judges would be much more accepting of arguments that Mr Khadr was a child soldier acting in self-defence during wartime.

Soon after the CBA convention, opposition leader Stéphane Dion threw the "Khadr effect" to the wind, announcing his intention to meet with Omar's lawyers and press for his repatriation. "It's not a matter of polls, it's not a matter of public opinion, it's a matter of rights,"[8] explained Mr Dion about the reasons for his personal involvement in the affair.

In addition to an increase in domestic activism on the Khadr file, Britain's law societies called on Canada to defend the rights of Omar in late 2007, pointing out the obvious – a fifteen-year-old Canadian citizen had been detained for five years, subjected to torture and interrogations without the right to silence or legal advice, and was facing a war-crimes trial before a US military commission whose rules were stacked in favour of a guilty verdict. While the US Supreme Court had ruled that juveniles could no longer face the death penalty, the American government declared that even if Omar was not found guilty, it may continue to hold him indefinitely. International law experts pointed out that Omar would be the first child soldier to face a trial in the West.

In a joint letter to Prime Minister Harper, Britain's General Council of the Bar, the Law Society, the Criminal Bar Association, the Commonwealth Lawyers' Association and the Bar Human Rights Committee wrote: "the lengthy detention, and putting on trial for war crimes, of someone who appears to be a 'child soldier' is contrary to the special protection to which Khadr is entitled."[9]

While the Harper government maintained a steely silence, it was faced with the embarrassing disclosure that an internal Foreign Affairs document placed the United States on a list of countries suspected of torturing prisoners – based on the prison at Guantanamo Bay where Canadian Omar Khadr is being held. Not surprisingly, US

Ambassador David Wilkins was indignant, demanding immediate removal of this reference.

Further international calls for the repatriation of Omar came in February of 2008 when Human Rights Watch, Amnesty International, the Coalition to Stop the Use of Child Soldiers, and Human Rights First asked Mr Harper to formally request that the United States either try Mr Khadr under juvenile justice rules or send him back to Canada. In addition, leaders of bar associations in Canada, the UK and France pointed out that the US *Military Commissions Act* of 2006 wrongly subjects individuals to trial by military commission solely on the basis of their status as aliens, noting that US citizens are not subject to its provisions.

That same month, another bombshell emerged in Omar's case. The military prosecutor inadvertently revealed that a key eyewitness to the murder of Lieutenant Speer did not actually see Omar throw a grenade at the medic. Rather, the eyewitness felt that an older fighter, who was present in the vicinity, threw the grenade. For years, the official American story was that Omar Khadr was the only combatant alive in the compound at the time of the medic's death, and that Omar's suspension of rights was justified based on his alleged battlefield actions. This official version was now fully in doubt and fuelled further calls for repatriation.

Still the Harper government continued to insist that the process should be allowed to continue – a process that was never fair to begin with, where a minor citizen of Canada was being degraded through a long, painful incarceration during which his basic human rights were suspended.

This strident approach flew in the face of many legal opinions. Omar Khadr was a "child" under the terms of the UN *Convention on the Rights of the Child* and his trial as a child soldier is prohibited under international humanitarian law, which regards a child soldier as a victim to be rehabilitated, rather than a perpetrator to be prosecuted. Senator Roméo Dallaire later publicly reiterated this point. Moreover, the trial of Omar Khadr constitutes a violation of the fundamental principles of law, including arbitrary and illegal detention; denial of procedural due process; the absence of the presumption of innocence; denial of the right to counsel; denial of the right to trial within a reasonable time before a fair and impartial tribunal; coerced interrogation, and cruel and unusual punishment in detention.

Irwin Cotler, who was Justice Minister during the detention of Omar, broke his silence in 2008 by pointing out that the US *Military Commissions Act* of 2006 criminalizes certain conduct for the first time and applies the law retroactively; it fails to meet the requirements of the Geneva Convention Relative to the Treatment of Prisoners of War; it permits military commissions to consider coerced statements; and it denies defence counsel access to evidence, which may be essential to a proper defence on the basis of national security.

Canadian politicians finally mustered enough courage to intervene in the case. At a news conference in late February, MPs from the Liberal Party, the NDP, and the Bloc Québécois joined Mr Khadr's US military lawyer, Lieutenant-Commander Bill Kuebler, to demand the return of Omar Khadr. Admitting that they had previously failed to protect the rights of Omar, and fully aware of the unpopularity of the Khadr name, the MPs made it clear that the issue at hand was a restoration of basic human rights and a fair, judicial process for the young man.

Throughout the spring, calls grew louder for the return of Omar to Canada.

The growing clamour was punctuated by the March 2008 revelation by the Guantanamo military commission that suggested evidence-tampering by US government officials during the initial period of Omar's imprisonment. One day after the fateful battle on July 27, 2002, a US commander at the scene wrote in a report that the assailant of Sgt Speer had been killed; in another version of the report (written several months later), someone had changed the word "killed" to "engaged." If the assailant had been killed, then Omar could in no way be charged with murder. Despite this latest revelation, the Harper government insisted on letting the Guantanamo "justice" system take its course.

In May 2008, a US military judge denied a defence motion to dismiss charges against Omar because of his age at the time of his alleged offences.

Then, in a stunning judgement in June, the US Supreme Court ruled that terrorist suspects imprisoned at Guantanamo were allowed to fight for their rights in the US. This was in direct rebuke to President George Bush who had announced the nature of the military tribunal on Nov. 13, 2001 in these terms: "It is not practicable to apply the principles of law and the rules of evidence generally recognized in the trial of criminal cases in the United States district courts."[10]

Another key turning point in the battle of public opinion occurred in July, when videotapes of Omar's interrogation in 2003 by CSIS agents were released – by order of the Canadian Supreme Court. The release followed a 9-0 ruling by the Supreme Court of Canada that the *Canadian Charter of Rights and Freedoms* may apply when Canada is complicit in human-rights violations affecting a Canadian abroad.

Let's also remember that the US Supreme Court has ruled on three separate occasions that Guantanamo detentions violate the US Constitution. United Nations human-rights experts have said the same with respect to international legal standards. President-elect Barack Hussein Obama, Hillary Clinton, and John McCain have all called for Guantanamo to be shut down. In 2005, a Canadian federal court concluded that the "conditions at Guantanamo Bay do not meet Charter standards."[11]

All experts agree that regardless of the outcome of this case, it will be precedent-setting. If his trial proceeds and Omar is convicted, Canadian law allows him to appeal to Ottawa to let him serve the remainder of his sentence at home. Under the *International Transfer of Offenders Act*, the Public Safety Minister may consent to such a transfer.

Questions for the Future

So, what are we to make of government complicity in a process that is widely recognized as a travesty of justice? Is it simply a combination of racism and Islamophobia, as some suggest? The evidence indeed indicates that suspicion of the "other" has played a role in the suspension of civil liberties of Muslim and Arab men by Canadian security, intelligence, and political officials.

If we look to history, we do see a disturbing pattern, wherein the collective rights of an identifiable group were trampled in the name of security. During both world wars, Canadian government policy makers did not hesitate to intern Canadians of diverse ethnicities, including Japanese, German, and Ukrainian Canadians. Lives were destroyed in the name of security. Similarly, with the operation of the *War Measures Act*, hundreds of innocent Quebecers were rounded up and imprisoned on suspicion of *indépendentiste* leanings. And since the events of September 11, 2001, Muslims and Arabs have also come under suspicion – especially if they speak out against American or Canadian foreign policy. And while there are no blanket internment policies this time, it is clear that the creation and maintenance of Guantanamo, and other security and intelligence strategies, operate as a form of severe internment that disregards the basic human rights of many Muslims. Recall that senior RCMP intelligence agents assigned to monitor Arar, told the O'Connor Inquiry that "all caveats were down"[12] – meaning that safeguards were cast aside in the pursuit of terrorism suspects.

While Prime Minister Jean Chrétien showed true leadership in keeping Canada out of the immoral Iraq invasion of 2003, the silence and complicity of the ruling Liberal government in the affairs of Maher Arar, Abdullah Almalki, Ahmad El Maati, Muayyed Nureddin, and Omar Khadr is shameful.

The current Conservative regime – with its tough stance as a law-and-order party – has decided that security trumps human rights. It is safe to say that the New Conservative Party is the ideological cousin of the current US Republican administration; the Harperites will try their best not to embarrass the Bush regime. And the Conservatives know full well how to exploit the politics of fear – especially when it comes to Muslims. As written elsewhere in this volume, Prime Minister Harper appealed to the fear factor of the Quebec electorate when he waded into the manufactured veiled vote *brouhaha*.

The web of deceit surrounding Omar's case has been woven with many strands, including Islamophobia and racism. However, it seems that the strongest impetus by successive Liberal and Conservative governments to keep a child-soldier imprisoned in Guantanamo, has been the desire to acquiesce to American demands about security. Our sovereignty has been compromised by political considerations, thus leading many to ask: "What is the value of my Canadian citizenship?"

And what has been the reaction of Canadian Muslims to these events? Initially, there was fear of speaking out against injustice lest one be labelled a terrorist sympathizer. We must remember that a large portion of the Canadian Muslim community are immigrants, and are acutely aware of possible reprisals by both governments of their countries of origin and the Canadian government. Also, many do not know how to navigate the Canadian legal and political systems. A few national Muslim community institutions have emerged within the last ten years – however, many are still experiencing growing pains. Nonetheless, Muslims need to stand up for justice in a balanced way that protects human rights and security.

It is civil society that has shown true strength of character during these troubled times. NGOs, human rights groups, journalists, and the courts have slowly, but surely, fought for justice for those wrongly treated. We cannot take the freedoms and rights that we have for granted. For these have been established through hard work and sacrifice by many Canadians who preceded us. In one aspect, Canada is a compassionate meritocracy woven by the efforts of countless women and men. We must join together to uphold values that we cherish, such as freedom, genuine respect, and fairness.

In looking back, we see that dark episodes of ethnic profiling were punctuated by the enlightened efforts of those who fought back, leading to the evolution of social justice and law for the benefit of future generations. In the process, each group became further entrenched within the Canadian mosaic. At this point in Canadian history, Canadian Muslims and Arabs face the pernicious spectre of ethno-religious profiling and a devaluation of their citizenship. If we are to learn anything from history, it is that abuses of government power cannot be left unchallenged. Canadians of good conscience must join together to fight for the basic human dignity of their fellow citizens. With each fresh revelation about human rights abuses perpetrated by the Canadian government in the name of security, we must heighten our vigilance against abuses of power, and demand due process for those who are detained or exiled without charge. Let's take on this responsibility with confidence, tenacity and courage, remembering the Qur'anic verse: *God does not place a burden on anyone heavier than one can bear.*

Notes

Knowing the Universe in All its Conditions

I would like to acknowledge Naznin Virji-Babul, Farouk Mitha, Kutub Kassam, Amyn Sajoo and Aly Lakhani for challenging and encouraging me to put my thoughts down on paper, and for engaging me in insightful discussions that have helped sharpen the ideas presented here. I would like to dedicate this essay to the memory of my father, Amirali Premji Babul, who passed away a few months ago. He first started me on this journey.

1 Contrary to popular misconceptions, Muslims are not a monolithic people in their understanding of Islam. Rather, the unfolding of the timeless message of Islam, over time and as a result of a remarkable ethnic, linguistic, and cultural plurality that it embraces, has given rise to a breadth of interpretations, judicial preferences, and socio-political institutional arrangements. Shia Ismailism is one such response. For a brief introduction to the Shia Imami Ismaili community, the present and the 49th Imam of the Ismailis in direct lineal descent from Prophet Muhammed, Prince Karim Aga Khan, and the Ismaili concept of Imamat (qualified and rightly guided spiritual leadership) please see the following webpages:

http://www.akdn.org/about_imamat.asp
http://www.akdn.org/about_agakhan.asp
http://www.akdn.org/about_community.asp

2 Maurice Bucaille, *The Bible, The Qur'an and Science: The Holy Scriptures Examined in the Light of Modern Knowledge*, translated from the French by Alastair D Pannell and the author (Tripoli: Islamic Call Society, 1976).

3 The Holy Qur'an 55:37–38. These verses are commonly translated as "When the sky is rent asunder, and it becomes red like ointment: Then which of the favours of your Lord will ye deny? "A Yusuf Ali, *The Holy Qur'an: Translation and Commentary*,

2d ed. (American Trust Publications, 1977); or as "And when the heaven splitteth asunder and becometh rosy like red hide – Which is it, of the favours of your Lord, that ye deny?" MA Haleem Eliasii, *The Holy Quran: Transliteration in Roman Script* trans by Mohammed Marmaduke Pickthall (New Delhi: Kitab Bhavan, 2002).

[4] Richard C Lewontin, "The Wars over Evolution," *The New York Review of Books* 52 (2005): 16.

[5] Ebrahim Moosa, *Islam and Cultural Issues* (Victoria: University of Victoria, Centre for Studies in Religion and Society, 2002).

[6] Ebrahim Moosa's impressive credentials as a scholar include the alimiyya degree from Darul Ulum Nadwatul 'Ulama, one of India's foremost Islamic seminaries in the city of Lucknow, Uttar Pradesh, where he received extensive training in the traditional Islamic Sciences.

[7] The Holy Qur'an 39:17–18, as quoted in Ebrahim Moosa, *Islam and Cultural Issues*, 13.

[8] Speech by His Highness the Aga Khan at the opening session of an international colloquium titled "Word of God, Art of Man: The Qur'an and its Creative Expressions," held at the Institute for Ismaili Studies, London, UK, October 19, 2003.

[9] Ebrahim Moosa, *Islam and Cultural Issues*, 5.

[10] The Holy Qur'an 3:190–191 in A Yusuf Ali, *The Holy Qur'an: Translation and Commentary*, 2d ed. (American Trust Publications, 1977).

[11] John William Draper, *History of the Conflict Between Religion and Science* (New York: Appleton-Century-Crofts, 1874).

[12] J L Heilbron, *The Dilemmas of An Upright Man: Max Planck as Spokesman for German Science* (Berkeley and Los Angeles: University of California Press, 1986).

[13] M Wertheim, *Pythagoras' Trousers: God, Physics and the Gender Wars* (New York: WW Norton & Company, 1997), 71.

[14] Frank Wilczek, "Reasonably Effective: I. Deconstructing a Miracle," *Physics Today* 59, no.11 (2006): 8–9.

[15] Alice Calaprice, *The Quotable Einstein*, (Princeton: Princeton University Press, 1996).

[16] Eugene Wigner, "The Unreasonable Effectiveness of Mathematics in the Natural Sciences," *Communications on Pure and Applied Mathematics* 13, no.1 (1960): 1–14; reprinted in E P Wigner, *Symmetries and Reflections: Scientific Essays of Eugene P Wigner* (Bloomington: Indiana U Press, 1967).

[17] Quoted in Alan Lightman, *Sense of the Mysterious: Science and the Human Spirit* (New York: Pantheon, 2005), 66.

[18] E Salaman, "A Talk With Einstein," *The Listener* 54 (1955): 370–371. Quoted in

M Jammer, *Einstein and Religion: Physics and Theology* (Princeton: Princeton University Press, 1999). See also "Einstein's Unfinished Symphony," BBC television, http://www.bbc.co.uk/sn/tvradio/programmes/horizon/einstein_symphony_prog_summary.shtm

[19] Johannes Kepler, *Harmonices Mundi* (1618) – as quoted in Steven G Krantz & Brian E Blank, *Calculus: Multivariable* (2006). This was the book in which Kepler presented the third of his three laws that indicated a geometric basis for the motion of the planets in orbit around the sun. Initially, Kepler sought to describe the orbits as perfect circles, in keeping with the Pythagorean notion of heavenly spheres. The totality of the relationships he discovered, however, pointed to elliptical orbits, which nonetheless are geometric structures.

[20] A Einstein, "The World As I See It," *Forum and Century* 84 (1951): 193–194; reprinted in *Living Philosophies* (New York: Simon Schuster, 1931), 3–7, and more recently in A Einstein, *Ideas and Opinions*, ed. Carl Seelig (New York: Bonanza Books, 1954), 8–11.

[21] Alan Lightman, *Sense of the of the Mysterious: Science and the Human Spirit* (New York: Pantheon, 2005), 3–64.

[22] Charles Taylor, *A Secular Age* (Cambridge, Mass.: Havard University Press, 2007), 5.

[23] Aga Khan III, *Selected Speeches and Writings of Sir Sultan Muhammad Shah*, ed. KK Aziz (London: Kegan Paul International, 1997), 171, 866.

Islamic Theology and Moral Agency: Beyond the Pre- and Post-Modern

I would like to express my gratitude to Professors Benjamin Berger, Richard Bulliet, and Gabrielle Spiegel for their generosity and enthusiasm for this article. Their comments and responses to an earlier draft of this article contributed to its substantial improvement. Likewise my friend and colleague Sayeed Rahman offered a fresh set of eyes on this article, and shared keen insights that I greatly appreciate. I also want to thank Professor Natasha Bakht for inviting me to contribute to this volume, and for her encouragement of the ideas expressed herein. I alone remain responsible for any deficiencies or errors.

[1] Anver M Emon, "Enhancing Democracy, Respecting Religion: A Dialogue on Islamic Values and Freedom of Speech," in *Faith and Law: How Religious Traditions From Calvinism to Islam View American Law*, ed. Robert F Cochran (New York: New York University Press, 2007): 273–90; "Conceiving Islamic Law in a Pluralist Society:

History, Politics and Multicultural Jurisprudence," *Singapore Journal of Legal Studies* (December, 2006): 331–355; "On the Pope, Cartoons, and Apostates: Shari'a 2006," *Journal of Law and Religion* 22 no. 2 (2006–7): 303–321.

2 In this regard, there are various studies on meaning and agency that have contributed to the interest and aims of this article. For instance, see Charles Taylor, *Sources of the Self: The Making of the Modern Identity* (Cambridge, Mass.: Harvard University Press, 1989); Hans-Georg Gadamer, *Truth and Method*, trans. Joel Weinsheimer and Donald G Marshall, 2d ed. (New York: Continuum, 1989); Alasdair C MacIntyre, *Whose Justice? Which Rationality?* (Notre Dame: University of Notre Dame Press, 1989); idem., *After Virtue*, 2d ed. (Notre Dame: University of Notre Dame Press, 1984); Jules Coleman and Brian Leiter, "Determinacy, Objectivity, and Authority," *University of Pennsylvania Law Review* 142 (1993): 549–637; Gabrielle Speigel, *The Past as Text: The Theory and Practice of Medieval Historiography*, new ed. (Baltimore: John Hopkins University Press, 1999); idem, ed, *Practicing History: New Directions in Historical Writing* (London: Routledge, 2005).

3 Qur'an 14:4, 35:8, 74:31.

4 Qur'an 6:125. On this verse, see, Muhammad b. Jarir al-Tabari (d. 310/923), *Tafsir al-Tabari*, ed. Bashshar Awad Ma'ruf and 'Isam Faris al-Harastani (Beirut: Mu'assasat al-Risala, 1994), 3:345, who focuses on how being open to faith is different from being closed off to disbelief. He suggests that both are caused by God, but indicates that God responds to the intent of the individual. In other words, al-Tabari seems to find a middle ground between the free will and determinism position by inserting human intentionality as a basis for what is effectively God's act. See also 'Imad ad-Din Ibn Kathir (d.774/1373), *Mukhtasar Tafsir Ibn Kathir, ed.* Muhammad al-Sabuni, 7th ed. (Beirut: Dar al-Qur'an al-Karim, 1981), 1:617–618, who writes that the verse is meant to indicate that God makes Islam easier for the one who is guided. Both authors, however, arguably illustrate an angst about the willfulness of one's faith commitments. For an exegesis of this verse that explicitly takes into account its implications on the debate on free will and determinism, see Fakhr al-Din al-Razi (d. 606/1210), *al-Tafsir al-Kabir* (Beirut: Dar Ihya' al-Turath al-'Arabi,1999), 5:137–145.

5 See, for example, Qur'an 2:29, 6:73, 14:19, 14:32, 25:2, 25:59.

6 Qur'an 2:286. On this verse, see al-Zamakhshari, *al-Kashshaf*, 1:408; al-Tabari, *Tafsir al-Tabari*, 2:199; Fakhr al-Din al-Razi, *al-Tafsir al-Kabir*, 3:115–125. For other verses conveying a similar theme, see Qur'an 34:4–5, 99:6–7.

7 The philosopher and jurist Ibn Rushd (Averroes) (d. 595/1198) explained that the debate between the theological schools on this issue was directly related to the inconsistency among the verses noted above. Ibn Rushd, *Manahij al-Adilla fi 'Aqa'id*

al-Milla, ed. Mahmud Qasim (Cairo: Maktabat al-Anjlu al-Misriyya, 1955) 107. For a translation of this text, see, Ibrahim Najjar, *Faith and Reason in Islam: Averroes' Exposition of Religious Arguments* (Oxford: Oneworld Publications, 2001). As discussed below, Ibn Rushd does not see a contradiction in these verses. Rather, he views the individual as able to make choices in the light of external causes that condition his context and scope of choice.

[8] This view seems to have been held by an earlier group called the Qadariyya. Richard C Martin et al, *Defenders of Reason in Islam: Mu'tazilism from Medieval School to Modern Symbol* (Oxford: Oneworld Publications, 1997), 25; Harry Austryn Wolfson, *The Philosophy of the Kalam* (Cambridge: Harvard University Press, 1976), 619–620; W Montgomery Watt, *The Formative Period of Islamic Thought* (Oxford: Oneworld Publications, 1998), 82–112. The term 'qadariyya' however seems to have been a pejorative term used by both sides of the debate to denigrate the other. For example, Abu Hanifa refers to the Qadariyya and the Mu'tazila as holding the same position on the characteristics of God. Abu al-Hasan al-Ash'ari calls his opponents on the doctrine of free will and determinism the 'qadariyya'. Abu al-Hasan 'Ali b. Isma'il al-Ash'ari, *Kitab al-Lum'a*, ed. 'Abd al-'Aziz 'Izz al-Din al-Sirwan (n.p.: Dar Libnan, 1987), 131. On the other hand, the Zaydi-Mu'tazili al-Qasim al-Rassi (d. 246/860), calls the determinists the 'qadariyya.' Al-Qasim al-Rassi, 'Kitab al-'Adl wa al-Tawhid wa Nafy 'an Allah al-Wahid al-Hamid,' in *Rasa'il al-'Adl wa al-Tawhid, ed.* Muhammad 'Imara (Cairo: Dar al-Shuruq, 1987), 146.

[9] Martin et al, *Defenders of Reason*, 25.

[10] Majid Khadduri, *The Islamic Conception of Justice* (Baltimore: Johns Hopkins University Press, 1984).

[11] For a biography of al-Ash'ari, see Abu al-'Abbas Ahmad b. Muhammad b. Ibrahim b. Abi Bakr b. Khallikan, *Wafayat al-A'yan wa Anba' Abna' al-Zaman*, eds. Yusuf 'Ali Tawil and Maryam Qasim Tawil (Beirut: Dar al-Kutub al-'Ilmiyya, 1998), 3:249–250; Shams al-Din Muhammad b. Ahmad b. 'Uthman al-Dhahabi, *Siyar A'lam al-Nubala'*, 4th ed. (Beirut: Mu'assasat al-Risala, 1986), 15:85–90; Abu al-Falah 'Abd al-Hayy b. al-'Imad, *Shadharat al-Dhahab fi Akhbar man Dhahab* (Beirut: Dar al-Kutub al-'Ilmiyya, n.d.), 2:303–305; W Montgomery Watt, 'al-Ash'ari,' in *Encyclopaedia of Islam*, eds. HAR Gibb et. al., rev ed. (Leiden: Brill), 1:694.

[12] For a general discussion of the Ash'ari position on acquisition, see Ibn Rushd, *Minhaj al-Adilla*, 110–111; W Montgomery Watt, 'Ash'ariyya,' in *Encyclopaedia of Islam*, eds. HAR Gibb et al, 1:696; Wolfson, *The Philosophy of the Kalam*, 684–710;

[13] Different historical sources proffer three potential years of his death: 943, 944 and 947. W Madelung, "al-Maturidi, Abu Mansur Muhammad b Muhammad b

Mahmud al-Samarkandi," *Encyclopaedia of Islam*, eds. P Bearman et al (Leiden: Brill, 2008), 6:846.

[14] W Montgomery Watt, *The Formative Period of Islamic Thought* (1973; Oxford: Oneworld Publications, 1998), 315.

[15] Abu Hanifa, *al-Fiqh al-Akbar*, 4.

[16] Notably, Ibn Rushd suggested that the difference between the Maturidis and the Mu'tazilites is terminological (*lafti*). Ibn Rushd, *Minhaj al-Adilla*, 115.

[17] Ibn Rushd, *Minhaj al-Adilla*, 110–112. Accounts of this debate are well documented both by premodern Muslim authors, as well as modern intellectual historians of the Islamic world. On premodern writers, see Abu al-Fath Muhammad b 'Abd al-Karim b. Abi Bakr Ahmad al-Shahrastani, *al-Milal wa al-Nihal*, eds. Amir 'Ali Mahna and 'Ali Hasan Fa'ur (Beirut: Dar al-Ma'rifa, 1996); 'Abd al-Qahir b Tahir b Muhammad al-Tamimi, *al-Farq bayna al-Firaq* (Beirut: Dar al-Kutub al-'Ilmiyya, n.d.); Abu Muhammad 'Ali b Ahmad b Hazm al-Zahiri, *al-Fasl fi al-Milal wa al-Ahwa' wa al-Nihal* (Beirut: Dar al-Fikr, n.d.); Abu Muhammad al-Yamani, *'Aqa'id al-Thalath wa Saba'in Firaq*, ed. Muhammad b 'Abd Allah Zarban al-Ghamidi (Medina: Maktabat al-'Ulum wa al-Hikam, 1414 AH). For contemporary accounts of this debate, see Tilman Nagel, *The History of Islamic Theology: From Muhammad to the Present*, trans. Thomas Thornton (Princeton: Markus Wiener Publishers, 2000); W Montgomery Watt, *Islamic Philosophy and Theology: An Extended Survey* (Edinburgh: Edinburgh University Press, 1985), 27–28, 50–51; Wolfson, *The Philosophy of the Kalam*, 601–719.

[18] Ibrahim Najjar, trans., *Faith and Reason in Islam: Averroes' Exposition of Religious Arguments* (Oxford: Oneworld Publications, 2001), 108.

[19] Ibn Rushd, *Minhaj al-Adilla*, 119.

[20] See for instance, William H Sewell, "A Theory of Structure: Duality, Agency and Transformation," in *Practicing History: New Directions in Historical Writing after the Linguistic Turn*, ed. Gabrielle Spiegel (London: Routledge, 2005), 143–165, for a compelling discussion of structure and agency in historical theory.

[21] For an introduction to the relationship between ethical theory and legal analysis, see Anver M Emon, "Natural Law and Natural Rights in Islamic Law," *Journal of Law and Religion* 20 no. 2 (2004–5): 351–395. While I have argued that Islamic natural law jurisprudence reflects a relationship between ethical and legal inquiry, that is not to say that law and morality are one and the same thing. For an important debate on the relationship between law and morality, see Patrick Devlin, *The Enforcement of Morals* (London: Oxford University Press, 1965); HLA Hart, *Law, Liberty and Morality* (Stanford: Stanford University Press, 1963).

[22] Taqi al-Din Ahmad B. Taymiyya, *Ihtijaj bi al-Qadar* (Cairo: al-Matba'a al-Salafiyya, 1394 AH) 6.
[23] Ibn Taymiyya, *Ihtijaj bi al-Qadar*, 6.
[24] Ibn Taymiyya, *Ihtijaj bi al-Qadar*, 6.
[25] Ibn Taymiyya, *Ihtijaj bi al-Qadar*, 6.
[26] Ibn Taymiyya, *Ihtijaj bi al-Qadar*, 6.
[27] Abu 'Abd Allah Muhammad b. 'Abd Allah al-Hakim al-Nisaburi, *al-Mustadrak 'ala al-Sahihayn* (Beirut: Dar al-Ma'rifa, 1998), 2:369, who related the tradition as narrated by Abu Sa'id al-Khudri.
[28] Najm al-Din al-Tufi, "*al-Hadith al-Thani wa al-Thalathun,*" in Mustafa Zayd, *al-Maslaha fi al-Tashri' al-Islami wa Najm al-Din al-Tufi*, 2d ed. (n.p.: Dar al-Fikr al-'Arabi, 1964), 205–240, 207.
[29] Al-Tufi, "*al-Hadith al-Thani wa al-Thalathun,*" 208.
[30] Al-Tufi, "*al-Hadith al-Thani wa al-Thalathun,*" 209.

Islamic Authority: Changing Expectations Among Canadian Muslims

[1] This project has been primarily funded by the Social Sciences and Humanities Research Council of Canada.

[2] The scope of this short chapter does not permit the author to conduct a full discussion of tradition and modernity, which are not viewed as irreconcilable polar opposites but as working in relation to each other (see Karim, 2002, 37–45).

[3] "The core of dominant Muslim discourses, established in the three centuries after the death of the prophet Muhammad in 632, has come historically to be used by hegemonic groups within Muslim societies to maintain their respective dominance. Over time, these discourses have become part of the orthodox understanding of Muslim creed and history and are broadly subscribed to not only by the political and religious elites but even militants who oppose the hegemony of these sections of society. Whereas the positions of the Islamists do form *oppositional* Muslim discourses, they do not seem to provide viable answers for the contingencies of technological society. More profound and practical Muslim proposals for countering Eurocentric influences and ensuring a modernity that is authentically Islamic have come from the *alternative* writings in contemporary times of such scholars as Muhammad Iqbal, Ali Shariati, Fazlur Rahman, Akbar Ahmad, Fatima Mernissi, Abdullahi An-Na'im, Aziz Al-Azmeh, Mohammed Arkoun, and Aziz Esmail, deriving from their familiarity with Islamic as well as Northern thought" (Karim, 2003, 8).

⁴ "... the ulama, in whatever stated form they functioned, came to have, in a wide and vague fashion, the ultimate decision on all questions of constitution, law and theology" (MacDonald, 1953, 599).

⁵ "'Islamism' and 'Islamist' rather than 'fundamentalism' and 'fundamentalist' (terms whose etymological roots like in Christian contexts) are used . . . to refer to those Muslims who adopt an ideologically reformist stance which promotes a return to an imagined ideal from the Muslim past. There is not only a geographic and cultural diversity among Islamists but also in their beliefs about establishing a utopic Islamic society and in their tactics" (Karim, 2003, 10).

⁶ Shia communities tend to have more centralized structures of authority than Sunnis. The Ismailis have a well-defined transnational network of institutions, which are also present in Canada (see Aga Khan IV circa 1998).

⁷ For a discussion on the failure of the traditionally trained religious Muslim leadership to comprehend contemporary conditions, see Zaman (2002, 181–91).

⁸ Yusuf and Shakir are affiliated with the Zaytuna Institute in California.

⁹ A number of the older respondents noted that they had accepted religious explanations from imams in home countries at face value, but their children who had been exposed to contemporary Western criticality were not satisfied with this approach and sought answers based on logic and evidence. Tariq Ramadan (2004) has written about the distinctness of "Western Muslims."

A Case of Mistaken Identity: Inside and Outside the Muslim Ummah

¹ "Islam is a Faith of Reason," *Spiegel Online International* (October 12, 2006).

² Tarek Fateh, "Yasmin Ratansi – Canada's First Muslim MP," *Toronto Star*, 23 July 2004.

³ "Speak . . ." in *O City of Lights, Faiz Ahmed Faiz: Selected Poetry and Biographical Notes*, ed. Khalid Hasan, trans Daud Kamal and Khalid Hasan (Oxford: Oxford University Press, 2006), 152.

Victim or Aggressor? Typecasting Muslim Women for Their Attire

¹ *Dahlab v Switzerland*, no. 42393/98 (15 February 2001). The hijab literally means both "modesty" and the "veil" in Arabic. There are a variety of different forms of veils

ranging from the headscarf (the hijab) to the face veil (the niqab) to the burqa which covers the entire face and body.

² *Police v Razamjoo*, (2005) DCR 408 (DCNZ) [*Razamjoo*].

³ *Sahin v Turkey* [GC], no. 44774/98, (2005) 41 EHRR 8.

⁴ *Muhammad v Enterprise Rent-a-Car*, No. 06-41896-GC (Mich. 31st Dist. Ct. Oct. 11, 2006).

⁵ Sherene H Razack, *Casting Out: The Eviction of Muslims from Western Law & Politics* (Toronto: University of Toronto Press, 2008).

⁶ The tragic death of Mississauga teenager Aqsa Pervez was widely reported in the media as the result of her fundamentalist father's reaction to her refusal to wear the hijab. Tarek Fatah and Farzana Hassan "The Deadly Face of Muslim Extremism," *National Post*, 12 December 2007; online: http://www.nationalpost.com/todays_paper/story.html?id=162281.

⁷ Abdelatif was perplexed that the Bordeaux Detention Centre had said nothing about their concerns with her headscarf earlier. Her application included a complete portfolio with photos of her wearing the hijab and yet she was not told of the problem until after she had completed her initial examination and was a week into her training. "They just told me you either take it off, or you can't work here." "Quebec firm on hijab ban for prison guards," *CTV News* (15 March 2007); online: http://www.ctv.ca/servlet/ArticleNews/story/CTVNews/20070315/hijab_que_070315/20070315?hub=TopStories.

⁸ "Muslim Girl Ejected from Tournament for Wearing Hijab," *CBC News* (25 February 2007); online: http://www.cbc.ca/canada/story/2007/02/25/hijab-soccer.html.

⁹ "Rule Against Hijab Stands: World Soccer Body" *CBC News* (3 March 2007); online: http://www.cbc.ca/canada/ottawa/story/2007/03/03/fifa-hijab.html.

¹⁰ *Ibid*. Indeed hijabi soccer players make up a large group of the world's elite-level athletes.

¹¹ "FIFA Hijab Ruling Deserves Red Card," *The Edmonton Journal* (6 March 2007); online: http://www.canada.com/edmontonjournal/news/opinion/story.html?id=59f06a4e-5043-4c33-b82a-acd43195b3e4.

¹² "Quebec Muslim Girls Banned from Tae Kwon Do Tournament," *The Council on American-Islamic Relations Canada* (15 April 2007); online: http://www.caircan.ca/itn_more.php?id=P2901_0_2_0_C.

¹³ "World Taekwondo Federation Upholds Quebec's Hijab Ban," *CBC News* (15 May 2007); online: http://www.cbc.ca/canada/montreal/story/2007/05/15/qc-taekwon0515.html.

¹⁴ Sarah Elgazzar, CAIR-CAN spokeswoman in "Quebec Muslim Girls Banned

from Tae Kwon Do Tournament" *The Council on American-Islamic Relations Canada* (15 April 2007); online: http://www.caircan.ca/itn_more.php?id= P2901_0_2_0_C.

[15] "Sensible Thinking on Hijab," *Edmonton Journal* (20 December 2007); online: http://www.canada.com/edmontonjournal/news/opinion/story.html?id=659 772ea-e778-45c0-98cb-2d1fff2a3157.

[16] Alan Cowell, "Blair Criticizes Full Islamic Veil as 'Mark of Separation,'" *New York Times*, 18 October 2006; online: http://www.nytimes.com/2006/10/18/world/europe/18britain.html?_r=1&oref=slogin.

[17] Stephen Brown, "Muslim Women Shouldn't Hide Behind Veil, Italian PM Says," *Toronto Star*, 18 October 2006, A2.

[18] *Ibid.*

[19] "Dutch Propose Burka Ban in Public," *Globe and Mail*, 17 November 2006; online: http://www.theglobeandmail.com/servlet/story/RTGAM.20061117.wburqaban17/BNStory/International/home; "Dutch Cabinet Decides Against Burqa Ban," *Radio Netherlands Worldwide*, 22 January 2008; online: http://www.radionetherlands.nl/news/international/5611093/Dutch-cabinet-decides-against-burqa-ban.

[20] Tu Thanh Ha, "Boisclair Vows to Change Quebec Voting Rule," *Globe and Mail*, 23 March 2007; online: http://www.globeandmail.com.

[21] "Muslim Voters Required to Remove Face Coverings" *CTV News*, 23 March 2007; online: http://www.ctv.ca/servlet/ArticleNews/story/CTVNews/20070323/elections_muslim_070323/20070323?hub=QPeriod. See also, "Muslim Women Will Have to Lift Veils to Vote in Quebec Election," *CBC News*, 23 March 2007; online: http://www.cbc.ca/canada/quebecvotes2007/story/2007/03/23/qc-niqab20070323.html.

[22] *House of Commons Debates*, No. 016 (14 November 2007) at 873, 875 (Mr Paul Dewar). As MP Brian Murphy noted, "There are no complaints arising from the incidents that were of such widespread and common occurrence according to the government so as to cause us to be sitting here as a priority debating Bill C-6." *House of Commons Debates*, No. 016 (14 November 2007) at 867.

[23] *Canada Elections Act*, SC 2000, c. 9.

[24] Law and Government Division, Legislative Summary LS-572E, "Bill C-6: An Act to Amend the Canada Elections Act (Visual Identification of Voters)" by Sebastian Spano, (Parliamentary Information and Research Service: Library of Parliament, 5 November 2007) at 2.

[25] "PM blasts Elections Canada Ruling on Veiled Voting," *CTV News*, 9 September 2007; online: http://www.ctv.ca/servlet/ArticleNews/story/CTVNews/20070909/harper_veils_070909/20070909?hub=TopStories.

26 "Visual Identification of Voters Bill C-6 Unfairly Targeting Muslim Women," *Hill Times*, 5 November 2007, 40.

27 "A Bad Bill on Veils," *Globe and Mail*, 30 October 2007, A24.

28 Raheel Raza, "Let's Pull the Veil off Our Minds," http://www.raheelraza.com/veils.htm.

29 "Canadian Muslim Leader Alleges Her Veil Views Sparked Vandalism" *Canadian Press*, 31 October 2006; online: http://sisyphe.org/article.php3?id_article=2451.

30 *Syndicat Northcrest v. Amselem*, 2004 SCC 47, [2004] 2 SCR 551 at paras. 46–47. In the New Zealand case of *Razamjoo, supra* note 2 at para. 67, Judge Moore similarly relied on the test of whether the claimant herself sincerely believed that the practice of wearing a burqa was required by her faith. Courts in the United States have taken a similar approach to the adjudication of religious belief. See *McMillan (aka Olugbala) v State of Maryland* 258 Md.147 (1970) at 153.

31 The argument in this section relies on a similar argument made by Carolyn Evans regarding conflicting stereotypes about Muslim women in two judgments of the European Court of Human Rights. See Carolyn Evans, "The 'Islamic Scarf' in the European Court of Human Rights," [2006] MelbJIL4; (2006) 7:1 *Melbourne Journal of International Law* 52.

Politics Over Principles: The Case of Omar Khadr

1 Heba Aly, "Canadian Languishes in Embassy in Sudan," *Globe and Mail*, 1 July 2008, A10.

2 Paul Koring, "Canada Feared US Backlash Over Man Trapped in Sudan," *Globe and Mail*, 24 July 2008.

3 Shephard, Michelle. *Guantanamo's Child: The Untold Story of Omar Khadr*. (Mississauga: John Wiley & Sons, 2008).

4 Allison Dunfield, "Khadr's Arrest Raises Serious Questions, Harper Says," *Globe and Mail*, September 2, 2002, and Clifford Krauss, "Canadian Teenager Held by US in Afghanistan in Killing of American Medic," *New York Times*, 14 September 2002.

5 "Canadian Officials Visited Teen Held by United States," *Globe and Mail*, February 22, 2003, A7.

6 Joe Clark, Lloyd Axworthy, Flora MacDonald, Bill Graham, John Manley, and Pierre Pettigrew, "Speak up, Mr Harper – Guantanamo is a disgrace," *Globe and Mail*, 1 February 2007.

7 Ian Austen, "Canada Reaches Settlement With Torture Victim," *New York Times*, 26 January 2007. See also: Gloria Galloway, "Harper Apologizes to Arar for Torture in

Syria," *Globe and Mail*, 26 January 2007.

[8] Colin Freeze, "Khadr Should Face Justice in Civilian Court, Dion Says," *Globe and Mail*, 19 September 2007.

[9] "Our Deafening Silence," *Globe and Mail* editorial, 2 January 2008.

[10] White House Press Release: "President Issues Military Order," 13 November 2001 [Presidential Order, Section 1(f)].

[11] *Khadr v Canada*, [2006] 2 FCR 506.

[12] "Report of the Events Relating to Maher Arar: Analysis and Recommendations," Commission of Inquiry into the Actions of Canadian Officials in Relation to Maher Arar, pp. 23, 108, 110, and 147.

Bibliography

Muslims and the Rule of Law

Adams, Michael. *Unlikely Utopia: The Surprising Triumph of Canadian Pluralism.* Toronto: Viking Canada, 2007.

Bielski, Zosia. "Ban Teachers From Religious Dress, Quebec Group Says," *National Post,* 9 October 2007.

Bouchard, Gerard and Charles Taylor. "Building the Future: A Time for Reconciliation. Abridged Report." Gouvernement du Quebec. 2008. http://www.accommodements.qc.ca/documentation/rapports/rapport-final-integral-en.pdf

Bouchard, Gerard and Charles Taylor. "Building the Future: A Time for Reconciliation. Complete Report." Gouvernement du Quebec. 2008. http://www.accommodements.qc.ca/documentation/rapports/rapport-final-integral-en.pdf

Boyd, Marion. *Dispute Resolution in Family Law: Protecting Choice, Promoting Inclusion.* 17 January 2005. http://www.attorneygeneral.jus.gov.on.ca/english/about/pubs/boyd/executivesummary.pdf

de Valk, Alphonse, ed. *Catholic Insight Magazine* (February 2008).

Esposito, John and Dalia Mogahed. *Who Speaks for Islam? What a Billion Muslims Really Think.* New York: Gallup Press, 2008.

Frank, Anne. *The Diary of a Young Girl.* Eds. Otto Frank and Mirjam Pressler. Translated by Susan Massotty. New York: Bantam Books, 1995.

Ha, Tu Thanh. "Islam Sparks Fiery Debate in Quebec," *Globe and Mail,* 24 October 2007.

Ha, Tu Thanh. "'We're Living in a Time of Hysteria,'" *Globe and Mail,* 21 November 2007.

Heinrich, Jeff. "Unions Against Religious Symbols." *Gazette,* 11 December 2007.

"Herouxville Wants Immigrants That Fit In With Its Citizens," *National Post,* 29 January 2007.

Iacobucci, Frank. "Internal Inquiry into the Actions of Canadian Officials in Relation to Abdullah Almalki, Ahmed Abou-Elmaati and Muayyed Nureddin." Government of Canada. 2008. http://www.iacobucciinquiry.ca/en/home.htm

Kymlicka, Will. "Disentangling the Debate." In *Uneasy Partners: Multiculturalism and Rights in Canada*, ed. Janice Stein. Waterloo, Ont: Wilfrid Laurier University Press, 2007.

Levesque, Lia. "Politician Wants Ban on Religious Clothing," *Toronto Star*, 26 September 2007.

Mishra, Pankaj. "A Paranoid, Abhorrent Obsession," *Guardian*, 8 December 2007.

"Montreal Cop in Trouble Over Controversial Song." *Canadian Press*, 28 January 2007.

"Controversial Columns Expose Jews to Hatred, BC Rights Tribunal Rules." *Canadian Press*. 3 February, 1999.

Pew Global Attitudes Project. Washington: Pew Research Center, 2007.

Siddiqui, Haroon. *Being Muslim*. Toronto: Groundwood Books, 2008.

Steyn, Mark. "The Future Belongs to Islam." *Maclean's*, 20 October, 2006.

Waggoner, Tim. "Pastor Fined $7,000 and Ordered to Publicly Apologize." VirtueonLine: http://www.lifesitenews.com/ldn/2008/jun/08060902.html

Towards a Dialogical Discourse for Canadian Muslims

Ali, Imam. *Nahj al-Balagha* (Path of Eloquence). Ed. Muhammad 'Abdeh. Beirut: Mu'asasat al-Ma'rif, 1996.

Dewar, Thomas. http://en.wikipedia.org/wiki/Tommy_Dewar

Huntington, Samuel. "The Clash of Civilizations?" *Foreign Affairs* 72.3 (1993): 22–49.

Kogawa, Joy. *Obasan*. 2d ed. Markham, Ontario: Penguin, 1983.

Malak, Amin. *Muslim Narratives and the Discourse of English*. New York: SUNY Press, 2005.

Razack, Sherene. "Imperilled Muslim Women, Dangerous Muslim Men and Civilized Europeans: Legal and Social Responses to Forced Marriages." *Feminist Legal Studies* 12 (2004): 129–174.

Rumi, Jalaluddin. *The Mevlevi Order*. The Threshold Society. 25 June 2008. http://www.sufism.org/society/mevlev.html

Said, Edward. "Intellectuals in the Post-Colonial World." *Salmagundi* 70–71 (1986): 44–64.

Islamic Authority:
Changing Expectations Among Canadian Muslims

Abou El Fadl, Khaled. *Speaking in God's Name: Islamic Law, Authority and Women.* Oxford: Oneworld, 2001.

Aga Khan IV. *The Constitution of the Shia Imami Ismaili Muslims.* Np, circa 1998.

Arkoun, Mohammed. *The Unthought in Contemporary Islamic Thought.* London: Saqi Books / Institute of Ismaili Studies, 2002.

Eickleman, Dale F and Jon W Anderson. "Redefining Muslim Publics." In *New Media in the Muslim World: The Emerging Public Sphere*, ed. Dale F Eickleman and Jon W Anderson. Bloomington: Indiana University Press, 2003.

Karim, Karim H. *Islamic Peril: Media and Global Violence.* Rev ed. Montreal: Black Rose Books, 2003.

Karim, Karim H. "Muslim Encounters with New Media: Towards an Inter-Civilizational Discourse on Globality?" *Islam Encountering Globalisation*, ed. Ali Mohammadi. London: Routledge, 2002.

MacDonald, D B. "Ulama." In *Shorter Encyclopaedia of Islam*, ed. by HAR Gibb and J H Kramers. Ithaca, NY: Cornell University Press, 1953.

Manji, Irshad. *The Trouble with Islam: A Wake-Up Call for Honesty and Change.* Toronto: Random House Canada, 2003.

The Muslim College. "Aims and Objectives." 2005. Accessed: 30 July 2008 http://www.muslimcollege.ac.uk/index.asp?query=aims

Ramadan, Tariq. *Western Muslims and the Future of Islam.* Oxford: Oxford University Press, 2004.

Zaman, Muhammad Qasim. *The Ulama in Contemporary Islam: Custodians of Change.* Princeton: Princeton University Press, 2002.

Contributors

ANAR ALI holds a Masters of Fine Arts from the University of British Columbia. Her work has appeared in various literary magazines and newspapers including the *New York Times*, the *Globe and Mail*, and *Inostrannaya* (Russia). Her first book *Baby Khaki's Wings* (Penguin 2006) was a finalist for the Trillium Book Award, the regional Commonwealth Writers Prize, Best First Book, and the Danuta Gleed Literary Prize. She was born in Tanzania, raised in Alberta, and now lives in Toronto.

ARIF BABUL is a physical cosmologist and a professor of physics and astronomy at the University of Victoria. His research focuses on elucidating the physical processes that govern the emergence and evolution of cosmic structure. He has authored or co-authored over a hundred research contributions and is a recipient of a number of honours including the prestigious Leverhulme Visiting Professorship at the Universities of Oxford and Durham in the UK and most recently, the University Distinguished Professorship, the University of Victoria's highest academic award. Beyond astrophysics, Dr Babul is an active participant in dialogues concerning nature and the place of Islamic civilization in the contemporary global setting.

NATASHA BAKHT is an assistant professor of law at the University of Ottawa. She was called to the bar of Ontario in 2003 and served as a law clerk to Justice Louis Arbour at the Supreme Court of Canada. Her research interests are generally in the area of law, culture and minority rights and specifically in the intersecting area of religious freedom and women's equality. Natasha has written extensively on the issue of religious arbitration in family law. Her probono work includes being active as a member of the Law Program Committee for the Women's Legal Education and Action Fund (LEAF). Natasha is also an Indian contemporary dancer and choreographer. She is the 2008 co-recipient of the KM Hunter Artists Award, presented to artists in Ontario who have begun to produce a body of work and make a significant mark in their field.

ANVER M EMON is an assistant professor at the Faculty of Law at the University of Toronto. Born, raised, and educated in the United States, Dr Emon moved to Toronto in 2005 to teach at the faculty of law, where he offers courses in tort law and varying topics in Islamic law. His research focus is on premodern and modern Islamic history, law, governance, and adjudication. He is also the founding editor of *Middle East Law and Governance: An Interdisciplinary Journal*.

KARIM H KARIM is the Director of Carleton University's School of Journalism and Communication. He was a Visiting Scholar at Harvard University's Divinity School and Department of Near Eastern Languages and Civilizations in 2004 and a Senior Research Fellow at the Institute of Ismaili Studies in London in 2005. Dr Karim received the inaugural Robinson Prize for excellence in communication studies for his book, Islamic Peril: Media and Global Violence. He holds degrees in Islamic and Communication studies from Columbia and McGill Universities.

AUSMA KHAN is the Editor-in-Chief of *Muslim Girl* magazine, a bi-monthly, North American publication. The first magazine to address a target audience of young Muslim women, Ms Khan describes *Muslim Girl* as an opportunity to reshape the conversation about Muslim women in North America. Ausma Khan holds a PhD in International Human Rights Law from Osgoode Hall Law School, Toronto, where her research specialization was humanitarian intervention and war crimes in the Balkans.

RUKHSANA KHAN is an award-winning children's author and storyteller. She was born in Lahore, Pakistan, and emigrated to Canada at the age of three with her family. She has nine books published with others under contract. Rukhsana is a mother of four, three girls and a boy, and a grandmother of one. To learn more about her please see her website: www.rukhsanakhan.com.

SHEEMA KHAN writes a monthly column for the *Globe and Mail* on issues pertaining to Islam and Muslims. She holds a PhD from Harvard University in Chemical Physics, along with numerous patents on drug delivery technology. She has served on the Board of the Canadian Civil Liberties Association (2004–2008), and is the founder of the Canadian Council on American-Islamic Relations (CAIR-CAN) and its former chair (2000–2005). She testified as an expert witness on Muslims in Canada before the O'Connor Inquiry, and has appeared before a number of parliamentary committees. In addition, she has spoken at numerous NGO conferences and government agencies on issues of security, civil rights and Muslim cultural practice. She is currently a patent agent in Ottawa.

AMIN MALAK, a graduate of the University of Baghdad, Carleton University, and the University of Alberta, is a professor of English and comparative world literature at Grant MacEwan College in Edmonton, Alberta. He has published articles in books and refereed journals on modern and contemporary fiction, postcolonial theory and literature, and Muslim cultural discourses. A recipient of faculty fellowships from the universities of Minnesota, Notre Dame, and Columbia, he has given thirty papers at conferences held in North America, Europe, the Middle East, and Asia. He is the author of *Muslim Narratives and the Discourse of English*, published by SUNY press in 2005.

SYED MOHAMED MEHDI received his PhD in philosophy from McGill University in 2008, writing his dissertation on conceptualisations of the contemplative life as a form of political action in Ancient and Modern political thought. Recently, his work has focused on Gandhian political philosophy and more broadly on the tension between ideals of personal moral transformation and participatory democracy. He is currently a professor of humanities and philosophy at Oakton Community College in Illinois, and was previously teaching at Montreal's John Abbott College. Since 2003 he has been closely involved in organizing and performing with Montreal's Kalmunity Vibe Collective, an independent group of musicians, writers and artists committed to the use of art for achieving social change. Some of his works in this context are collected in the *Talking Book Anthology* (Montreal: Cumulus Press, 2006).

HAROON SIDDIQUI is the editorial page editor emeritus and columnist for the *Toronto Star*, Canada's largest newspaper. He is a member of the Order of Canada and the Order of Ontario, and a recipient of an honourary doctorate from York University, the citation for which said that his work "helps in the creation and sustaining of a contemporary Canada." Long active in the Canadian Newspaper Association, Advertising Standards Canada, Canadian Civil Liberties Association, and Ontario Press Council, he helped change the media portrayal of minorities. A former president of PEN Canada, he is a director of International PEN, the writers' group that fights for freedom of expression through its 140 chapters in 101 countries.

Acknowledgements

I would like to thank the contributors to this collection for their patience, wisdom and thoughtful correspondences. My professional life usually has me working alone; this was a welcome change. I am also grateful to Nurjehan Aziz and TSAR Publications for presenting the opportunity to edit this book. It has been a wonderful learning experience. Finally, I would be nothing without my parents and brother and my perpetual editors and advisors Baidar Bakht, Vanessa Gruben, and Carmela Murdocca.